M000281032

TO

_____

FROM

_____

DATE

_____

LOVE ON

ONE MINUTE DEVOTIONS
FOR DOING GOOD
AND FEELING GREAT

DaySpring

LIVE YOUR FAITH

Love On: One Minute Devotions for Doing Good and Feeling Great
© 2018 DaySpring Cards, Inc. All rights reserved.
First Edition, November 2018

Published by:

P.O. Box 1010
Siloam Springs, AR 72761
dayspring.com

All rights reserved. No part of this book may be reproduced or transmitted in
any form or by any means, except by a reviewer, who may quote brief passages
in a review without permission in writing from the publisher.

Unless otherwise noted, Scripture quotations are taken from the Living Bible
with permission from Tyndale House Publishers, Inc., Wheaton, IL.

Scriptures marked THE MESSAGE are taken from The Message. © Eugene
Peterson. Permission from NavPress

Scriptures marked NIV are taken from THE HOLY BIBLE, NEW INTERNATIONAL
VERSION®, NIV® Copyright © 1973, 1978, 1984, 2011 by Biblica, Inc.® Used by
permission. All rights reserved worldwide.

Scriptures marked NKJV are taken from the New King James Version.
Copyright © 1982 by Thomas Nelson, Inc.

Scriptures marked NLT are taken from the Holy Bible, New Living Translation,
copyright © 1996, 2004, 2007 by Tyndale House Foundation. Used by
permission of Tyndale House Publishers, Inc., Carol Stream, Illinois 60188. All
rights reserved.

Written by Bonnie Rickner Jensen
Designed by Gearbox
Typeset by Jessica Wei
Printed in China
Prime: 10985
ISBN: 978-1-68408-572-9

JANUARY 1

*Regardless of what else you put on,
wear love.*
COLOSSIANS 3:14 THE MESSAGE

If love is what we live for,
Then the time to love is now.
It doesn't matter much the way;
What matters is the how.
Kindly, gently, fully, sweetly,
Selflessly and—WOW!—
Love with all your heart and soul.
Just please, please, *do it now!*

FATHER, LET MY WORDS AND ACTIONS
ON THIS NEW DAY—AND THROUGHOUT
THIS NEW YEAR— BE INFUSED WITH
YOUR LOVE!

JANUARY 2

If I gave everything I have...
but didn't love others,
it would be of no value whatever.
I CORINTHIANS 13:3

Love looks outward. It looks open-eyed but without judgment at the needs of others. It sees the hurting heart behind the hurtful action and the brokenness of the bully. Love is the healing balm for the bruised of the world. *Be an agent of healing today.*

FATHER, HELP ME TO SEE PEOPLE WITH YOUR EYES AND TO LOVE THEM WITH YOUR LOVE.

JANUARY 3

*Demonstrate the love and
kindness of the Lord.*
I SAMUEL 20:14

Here's something for your to-do list
today: *love.* Love is *kindness.* Love is
forgiveness. Love is *a smile.* Love is taking a deep breath and walking away
before you speak some not-so-nice
words. Love replaces bad with good and
bursts the bubble of fear. Today, let God
breathe His beautiful love into the world
through *you!*

FATHER, FILL ME WITH YOUR SPIRIT
AND USE ME TO BLESS OTHERS WITH
YOUR LOVE.

JANUARY 4

Let us stop just saying we love people;
let us really love them,
and show it by our actions.

1 JOHN 3:18

Go ahead and *love*. Right where you are,
do something that oozes love. Go to a
local elementary school and put money
on a child's lunch card. Let someone go
ahead of you in line at the grocery store.
Treat unkindness with a warm and sincere
smile. Small gestures can be *significant*
channels that broadcast God's love to
the world.

FATHER, MAY YOUR LOVE GUIDE AND
EMPOWER MY ACTIONS TODAY.

JANUARY 5

God chose us to be His very own
through what Christ would do for us;
He decided then to make us holy in His eyes,
without a single fault—
we who stand before Him covered with His love.
EPHESIANS 1:4

How we love others should *never* depend on how they love us, but instead only on how *Jesus* loves us. His all-encompassing, *unflinching* love—a divine love that covers us and makes us holy—won't draw back or falter no matter how we act or react, no matter what we do or don't do. Let's put some of this *no-matter-what* love in the world today and pay forward the Love that paid our sin-debt in *full* on the cross.

> FATHER, THANK YOU FOR SENDING JESUS TO DIE FOR OUR SINS AND THEN FOR CHOOSING ME TO BE YOUR CHILD. AND PLEASE USE ME TO LOVE WITH NO-MATTER-WHAT LOVE.

JANUARY 6

*Try to show as much compassion
as your Father does.*
LUKE 6:36

It'll leave a place better
Than *ever* it was.
It'll bring more good feelings
Than zealous applause!
It'll light up the world
For a heavenly cause
If we love with compassion
And *never* a pause!

FATHER, HELP ME LEAVE
THE AROMA OF LOVE AND COMPASSION
WHEREVER I GO.

JANUARY 7

*As we obey this commandment, to love one
another, the darkness in our lives disappears
and the new light of life in Christ shines in.*

I JOHN 2:8

Love brings beauty to broken places where
circumstances have left a life in shambles,
and hope has been hit hard. God is love,
and He is the *inexhaustible* Source of love
that enables us to love in those broken
places. In His power, we meet needs with
kindness, compassion, a shoulder to lean
on, a word of encouragement, and light
that will linger long after the need is met.

> FATHER, SHOW ME HOW TO SHINE THE
> LIGHT OF YOUR LOVE INTO EVERY LIFE
> I TOUCH.

JANUARY 8

Nothing can ever separate us from God's love.
ROMANS 8:38 NLT

Love. We can light the darkest night with it, start a hailstorm of hope with it, or move a mountain of malice with it. Not a weapon on earth can conquer God's powerful love—and God has put that powerful love in our hearts to use for His glory.

FATHER, PLEASE HELP ME BE A WISE AND EFFECTIVE STEWARD OF YOUR POWERFUL LOVE.

JANUARY 9

*If we love God, we will do
whatever He tells us to.
And He has told us from the very first
to love each other.*

II JOHN 1:6

Let it be your heart that listens
Well beyond the sound.
Let it tell you how to answer
When the words cannot be found.
Let it be your heart that hears
What *isn't* being said;
Through our hearts the love of God
Quietly is spread.

FATHER, PLEASE GIVE ME A HEART OF
LOVE AND THE DISCERNMENT TO SEE
WHAT PEOPLE AROUND ME NEED.

JANUARY 10

Love from the center of who you are;
don't fake it.
ROMANS 12:9 THE MESSAGE

Love breaks all barriers. It walks through walls of language, fear, race, and religion. It's strengthened when we exercise it, empowered when we use it, and enlarged when we invest it in others. It takes just a small measure to make a big difference... and the choice to love *always* brings life's greatest rewards.

FATHER, SHOW ME HOW TO LOVE WITHOUT FEAR AND WITHOUT HESITATION. HELP ME TO LOVE GENUINELY AS YOU DO.

JANUARY 11

Nothing will ever be able to separate us from the love of God demonstrated by our Lord Jesus Christ when He died for us.

ROMANS 8:39

How do we calm the crescendo of fears?
What do we do with a waterfall of tears?
Where do we go 'til the heaviness clears?
Who holds the lantern when hope disappears?

One who has felt every heartache unfurled...
One who has held all the weight of the world...
One who can heal what the darkness has hurled...
One who was Love, when hatefulness swirled.

FATHER, YOUR LOVE IS THE SOLACE FOR OUR SOULS AND THE HOPE FOR OUR HEARTS.

JANUARY 12

*Love the Lord and
follow His plan for your lives.*
JOSHUA 22:5

God's plan for us will always unfold according to His way of love. Content hearts and healthy souls come from clinging to Him, our love *lifeline*, and in turn extending His love to others. Giving love outwardly shapes our lives inwardly and keeps us in line with God's highest purpose.

FATHER, I'LL CLING TO YOU TODAY AND
PRAY YOUR LOVE GOES THROUGH ME
INTO EVERYTHING I DO.

JANUARY 13

Let us come boldly to the throne of our gracious God. There we will receive His mercy, and we will find grace to help us when we need it most.

HEBREWS 4:16 NLT

On some days it's just hard to love. It's difficult to give to others the love we've been given. God understands and therefore provides the *grace lens*. It has the power to change our perspective, soften our view, and remove anything that keeps our hearts from seeing another's worth. Such love is full of grace and free of condition—and it's the truest way for us to reveal to others the *realness* of God.

FATHER, WHEN I GROW WEARY OF LOVING, PLEASE—BY YOUR GRACE—RENEW MY HEART AND MY SOUL.

JANUARY 14

Fill all who love You with Your happiness.
PSALM 5:11

Happiness lives when we're happy to give! When we do a favor, act kindly, or help another, we make love tangible. When we see every opportunity to give as an opportunity for others to see God's love, the world becomes a richer place!

FATHER, OPEN MY EYES TO WAYS
I CAN EXPRESS YOUR LOVE TO OTHERS
AND THEREBY GIVE HAPPINESS
A HOME IN ME!

JANUARY 15

Be good friends who love deeply;
practice playing second fiddle.
ROMANS 12:10 THE MESSAGE

Putting others first more of the time puts more of God's joy in our lives! It's amazing how problems fade into the shadows and discouragement dims when we allow His love to illuminate our lives. We can then be both a light that shines on the good *in* others and the hands that do good *for* others—without much thought of self.

FATHER, TEACH ME, PLEASE, TO NOT ALWAYS PLACE MY NEEDS OR DESIRES FIRST. PLEASE GIVE ME A SERVANT HEART LIKE JESUS.

JANUARY 16

Blessed is the Lord, for He has shown me that His never-failing love protects me.

PSALM 31:21

Nothing will transform your heart like believing God loves you with all of His. Oh, on certain days—when it looks like everything you hope for is stuck somewhere between His hand and your current circumstances—you will find it harder to believe that His love is unfailing and unstoppable. But as you wait, know that His love *protects you*. He knows when it's best for His plans for you to unfold. In time you'll see God's love in the timing and recognize how He guided you every step of the way.

> FATHER, I BELIEVE YOUR LOVE PROTECTS ME, AND I KNOW THAT YOUR LOVE HAS SHAPED YOUR PERFECT WILL AND PERFECT TIMING FOR MY LIFE.

JANUARY 17

God is good, and He loves goodness.
PSALM 11:7

We can't love God with all of our hearts, souls, and minds if we aren't committed and *determined* to speak words and to live lives that reflect His goodness. It takes an act of our will to respond with love and goodness to every person we meet, whatever the circumstances. God will always help us. After all, our good God loves goodness.

FATHER, PLEASE USE MY WORDS
AND MY ACTIONS TO SPREAD THE
GOODNESS OF YOUR LOVE TODAY.

JANUARY 18

Praise the LORD, for He has shown me the wonders of His unfailing love.
PSALM 31:21 NLT

Love never fails, for God is love and love is *perfect.* We human beings mess up, certainly, but when we need forgiveness, we turn to *the wonders of [God's] unfailing love.* There we find ourselves face-to-face with God's mercy, His open arms, and the grace of a clean slate. May we respond with *praise... gratitude...* and *wonder* at the love that God *eternally* extends to us.

FATHER, THANK YOU FOR LOVING ME AND FOR RENEWING MY HEART'S DESIRE TO LOVE OTHERS.

JANUARY 19

If I understood all of God's secret plans and possessed all knowledge, and if I had such faith that I could move mountains, but didn't love others, I would be nothing.

I CORINTHIANS 13:2 NLT

Nothing else matters. Our intellect, our talents, our accomplishments, the measure of our faith—all this and everything else is worth nothing at all if we don't *love God and others.* Love simplifies our purpose: we are to love. Love narrows our focus: we are to keep our eyes on Jesus. So *every single day* may we love every person God puts in our path. Doing so is an act of obedience, but that extension of God's love just may put the ones we love on the path to *Him.*

FATHER, I WANT TO SHOW YOUR
LOVE TO OTHERS IN SIMPLE AND
SIGNIFICANT WAYS THROUGHOUT
EVERY DAY YOU GIVE ME ON
THIS EARTH.

JANUARY 20

*Love your enemies! Pray for those who
persecute you! In that way, you will be acting
as true children of your Father in heaven....
If you love only those who love you,
what reward is there for that?*

MATTHEW 5:44-46 NLT

God's love and our prayers perpetuate goodness more than anything else does. When we love, we are *giving* from the heart of God. When we pray, we are *going to* the heart of God—and both change us because we draw close to Him. He's our only hope of loving others despite our feelings and of forgiving others despite our pain. Besides, we're often in need of the same love and forgiveness from Him!

FATHER, I WANT TO BE A TRUE
REFLECTION OF YOU BY LOVING
AND FORGIVING, BY LIVING FREE OF
JUDGMENT AND FULL OF GRACE.

JANUARY 21

*Jesus replied, "Love the Lord your God
with all your heart, soul, and mind."*
MATTHEW 22:37

Our capacity to love is diminished by our
flesh that is constantly pushing its way to
the front of the line, bullying our desire to
love others by tempting us with self-cen-
teredness, pride, and unforgiveness. To be
all-in when it comes to loving others, we
need to love God with *all we are*. When He
gets first place in us—in our hearts, souls,
and minds—His love impacts everything
we do.

FATHER, ENABLE ME TO LOVE YOU
WITH ALL THAT I AM—AND TO LOVE
OTHERS WITH YOUR LOVE.

JANUARY 22

*The Word became human and
made His home among us.
He was full of unfailing love and faithfulness.*

JOHN 1:14 NLT

Love came down to earth to seek us: Jesus stepped from heaven into humanity to reveal *God's faithfulness* and meet once and for all our need for forgiveness. God's love transforms us into Christ's likeness, the true image of *who we are* and the best example of *why we're here*. Love is the reason to be alive, to be kind, to give, to do good, to forgive, to feel joy, and to thank God. *Nothing else in this world matters more.* Love is the only thing that means anything—because everything it touches leaves the fingerprint of God.

FATHER, LET YOUR LOVE OVERTAKE MY
HEART AND GUIDE MY ACTIONS TODAY,
THAT I MAY REFLECT THE LIGHT OF
YOUR GOODNESS AND GLORY.

JANUARY 23

You bless the godly, O Lord;
You surround them with Your shield of love.

PSALM 5:12 NLT

People only need a shield when they need protection, and the psalmist says we are surrounded by a shield of God's love. Turn in any direction and look for evidence of God's love. We won't avoid life's harshness, but God's love softens it. God's love also softens *our hearts.* In the midst of difficult days and our finicky feelings, let's remember God's shield of love around us and let us choose to be evidence of God's love for other people.

FATHER, THANK YOU FOR THE STRENGTH AND WARMTH OF YOUR LOVE. HELP ME GENEROUSLY SHARE IT WITH OTHERS.

JANUARY 24

Most of all, love each other
as if your life depended on it.
1 PETER 4:8 THE MESSAGE

We all have days when we stumble along, feeling like we don't get much, if anything, right. But love can interrupt any day and change *everything*. The moment we choose love, we choose God. We remember and receive afresh His love for us. Our day can change, and so can the days of those we choose to love with God's love. Love is always a win-win, so it's worth practicing often and wholeheartedly.

FATHER, KEEP MY FOCUS ON LOVE
TODAY—ON YOUR LOVE FOR ME
AND ON YOUR CALL TO ME TO LOVE
OTHERS—NO MATTER HOW I FEEL.
HELP ME CHOOSE YOU.

JANUARY 25

Give generously to others in need.
EPHESIANS 4:28 NLT

The enemy of our souls would like us to believe that giving drains us of our resources. If we give, he suggests, we lose time, money, or energy. But there is no truth in our enemy; there is no truth in what this deceiver—this liar—says. When we give, we spend something, yes, but we *never* lose. In God's economy, giving is gain. And if we ask God to guide our giving, we will gain the joy of obedience and the blessing of His using us in this world.

FATHER, LET ME GIVE
TO OTHERS WITH AN OPEN AND
GENEROUS HEART TODAY.

JANUARY 26

Love suffers long and is kind.
I CORINTHIANS 13:4 NKJV

We get weary. Emotionally exhausted at times. And the only way to recover is to go to the One who is Love: His grace is sufficient for every tired, weakened child of His. When our strength is *gone*, God's strength is *on*—and His strength empowers our hearts to love and our hands to kindness.

FATHER, I GO TO YOU FOR THE STRENGTH TO LOVE WELL AND TO SERVE WITH A HEART OF KINDNESS.

I am giving you a new commandment:
Love each other. Just as I have loved you,
you should love each other.

JOHN 13:34 NLT

Life's not in wishing we had
Or we *could.*
Life's in the love
We give out—and we *should!*
Think of the difference we'd make
If we *would*
Put others first and then
Do something good.
Love is a choice that
We make—and we should!
Others feel valued
And more understood
Hearts start to grow
And heart-growing is good!
If *one* thing changed *all* things,
Believe me, love *could.*

FATHER, YOU LOVE ME WITH KINDNESS
AND PATIENCE. ENABLE ME TO EXTEND
THAT SAME LOVE TO OTHERS.

JANUARY 28

Love makes up for practically anything.
I PETER 4:8 THE MESSAGE

We can't go wrong by loving people with God's love. If our actions are patient, kind, gentle, and generous, the power of God is released. If healing and hope aren't immediate, love is nevertheless planted, and good will come. When we scatter seeds of God's love, we enrich the soil of *our* souls, too, as we trust Him to guide and bless our sowing.

FATHER, YOUR LOVE MAKES
EVERY PERSON FEEL VALUABLE.
LET ME SOW SEEDS OF YOUR LOVE
ABUNDANTLY TODAY!

JANUARY 29

Be generous with the different things God gave you, passing them around so all get in on it...
That way, God's bright presence will be evident in everything.
I PETER 4:10-11 THE MESSAGE

Love shines differently through each of us. We might have a sense of humor that can fill a room with laughter. We might make others feel welcome with the warmth of our smile. Or maybe we're the friend who brings the chocolate and listens long and quietly. Love doesn't have only a single, one-size-fits-all expression. Love does have one *Source*, though—and He shines through us, His children, in a thousand ways!

FATHER, THANK YOU FOR MAKING
ME A UNIQUE EXPRESSION OF YOUR
AMAZING LOVE.

JANUARY 30

May those who love the Lord shine as the sun!
Judges 5:31

Travel the world.
Go high and go low.
Learn about people
And towns you don't know.
Take very little.
Think very big.
Stop and ask questions.
Be curious.
Dig.
Adventures you take
When you walk out your door
Will help you discover
That love matters *more!*

FATHER, LET MY LIFE SHINE THE LIGHT
OF YOUR LOVE WHEREVER I GO!

JANUARY 31

The eyes of the Lord are watching over those who rely upon His steady love.
PSALM 33:18

Steady love. That's what we can count on, because God's love is *never* interrupted by our lack of attention, our weaknesses, or our mistakes. We can depend on His love to be there for us—and ready for us to give away. Love only shortcircuits when we get *in* the way...with unforgiveness, impatience, busyness, and emotions. Today, let's rely on the steadiness of God's love to increase the selflessness of ours.

FATHER, YOUR LOVE IS SECURE. HELP
ME HOLD ON TO YOU AND REACH OUT
TO OTHERS.

FEBRUARY 1

Love your enemies. Let them bring out the best in you, not the worst. When someone gives you a hard time, respond with the energies of prayer, for then you are working out of your true selves, your God-created selves.

MATTHEW 5:44-45 THE MESSAGE

We're created in God's image and therefore can be a valuable expression of His love in this dark and lonely world. When we choose to love others despite the unlovable things they do, we choose the harder, *higher* road. That's one way the best in us—*God* in us—comes to light. Sharing God's love when it's hard changes us as well as those we choose to love... for the better.

FATHER, I'LL CHOOSE TO LOVE AND PRAY FOR OTHERS WHEN IT'S HARD TO DO BECAUSE IT'S WHAT YOU WANT, AND OBEDIENT LOVE GLORIFIES YOU.

FEBRUARY 2

O Lord! Look at me...
through eyes of mercy and forgiveness,
through eyes of everlasting love
and kindness.

PSALM 25:6

God always sees us through His lens of love because He *is* love! When He looks at us, He desires to be kind, to forgive, to have mercy on our weaknesses, and to *never give up on us*. Another of His heart-felt desires? That we see the people He brings into our lives through the same lens He looks at us. May we be kind, show mercy, and forgive. The more often we look at the world through God's lenses, the more often we share the divine love that has the power to change it.

FATHER, GIVE ME COMPASSION TO SEE
OTHERS THE WAY YOU SEE ME: WITH
LOVE AND KINDNESS.

FEBRUARY 3

God's unfailing love and faithfulness came through Jesus Christ.

JOHN 1:17 NLT

Jesus came to show the world God's love—and we are here to do the same! Every day will bring opportunities to share the amazing love God has poured into our lives, and these opportunities to selflessly extend His love to people will refine our reflection of Him. Love paints the purest image of God and leaves the most beautiful impression.

FATHER, REMIND ME OF YOUR UNFAILING LOVE TODAY, AND MAKE ME YOUR REFLECTION.

FEBRUARY 4

My love won't walk away from you.
ISAIAH 54:10 THE MESSAGE

God's love is not going anywhere. Ever.
It's hanging in there on the tough days,
comforting us in the sadness, standing
strong in our weakness, offering forgiveness of our sin, and holding us close...
always. God's love is sure; God's love is
eternal. Let's welcome ways to show people this kind of love and point them to
Him, the One whose love is perfect and
present. Always.

FATHER, MAY I BE VERY AWARE OF
YOUR LOVING PRESENCE WITH ME
TODAY. USE ME, I ASK, TO LAVISH YOUR
LOVE ON OTHERS.

FEBRUARY 5

We are able to hold our heads high no matter
what happens and know that all is well,
for we know how dearly God loves us.
ROMANS 5:5

We all know what it is to be treated in less-than-loving ways. But do we always—or ever—see that moment as our chance to dig deep and stand tall? Christlike love responds to anger and even to hatred with gentleness, quietness, and confidence rooted in God's love for us. Confident in His love, we can be careful with the careless and kind to those who aren't. Wielding love's power might not win arguments...but it will win hearts.

FATHER, YOUR LOVE IS MY ROCK AND
MY REASON TO LOVE OTHERS NO
MATTER HOW THEY TREAT ME.

FEBRUARY 6

*The wisdom that comes from heaven is first of
all pure and full of quiet gentleness. Then it is
peace-loving and courteous. It allows discussion
and is willing to yield to others; it is full of
mercy and good deeds. It is wholehearted and
straightforward and sincere.*

JAMES 3:17

That description of wisdom could be a
description of love. No wonder wisdom
from heaven inspires love for others. And
God's love touches hearts and is able to
change them. Nothing else that we say
or do makes as significant a difference in
someone's life as love does. So be the first
to smile. Listen quietly. Hug close. Speak
kindly. Serve humbly. Be creative as you
seek simple but special ways to love!

FATHER, SHOW ME EVERY
OPPORTUNITY TO SHARE
YOUR LOVE TODAY.

FEBRUARY 7

Nothing can ever separate us from God's love.
ROMANS 8:38 NLT

You are loved. You are loved with a love deeper than the oceans and higher than the sky. You are loved more faithfully than you can imagine. And you are loved and valued beyond measure by Your Creator just for being you. And You are more infinitely precious to Him than you can even comprehend. So, although we'll never perfect it this side of heaven, may we practice loving people every chance we get.

FATHER, MAKE ME AN INSTRUMENT IN YOUR MASTERFUL HAND, USING ME TRULY LOVE PEOPLE WITH YOUR LOVE.

FEBRUARY 8

Lord, let Your constant love surround us,
for our hopes are in You alone.
PSALM 33:22

No thing, no place, and no person can re-fuel our souls the way God and His love can. Also, we'll never know how to best love others if we don't turn to the One who created them. He is perfect, unparalleled Love. He knows exactly what every person's heart needs, and He can guide us in loving them. So let's turn to God in prayer today, fill up on His love, and with compassion and kindness, pour it out into the lives of others.

> FATHER, FILL ME WITH YOUR LOVE AND
> GIVE ME WISDOM ABOUT WHEN TO
> POUR IT OUT.

FEBRUARY 9

You love me so much!
You are constantly so kind!
PSALM 86:13

What a difference we'd make *in* our world if we were *constantly* kind! Even when we're tempted to act or respond otherwise because of our own woes and worries—or because of the way we're treated—choosing to be kind pulls us close the One who knows that *kindness and love go hand in hand*. And love is God's hand that moves us to bring some hope and even some healing to the lives of others.

FATHER, LET MY ACTIONS TODAY
BE ALIVE WITH YOUR LOVE
AND KINDNESS!

FEBRUARY 10

*Do not seek revenge or
bear a grudge against anyone...
but love your neighbor.*
LEVITICUS 19:18 NIV

Let the day begin by releasing any sense of self-pity, resentment, or annoyance. We can live grudge-free—forgiving others—because in God's eyes we're smudge-free—forgiven! New every morning are the soul-soothing waters of fresh mercy that God pours into our hearts to remind us that forgiveness and grace are ours to freely receive—and to *generously give*.

FATHER, THANK YOU FOR A CLEAN
START AND A CLEAN HEART. AND
THANK YOU FOR THIS DAY. HELP ME
OFFER TO OTHERS THE GRACE
YOU GIVE TO ME.

FEBRUARY 11

Love the Lord and
follow His plan for your lives.
Cling to Him
and serve Him enthusiastically.
JOSHUA 22:5

It can be hard to get excited in the murky mundane of life. The daily routine has a way of pushing us along robotically, tempting us to concentrate our energy on needs, not *nudges*. Is God asking us to do something? Has He put someone on our mind? If so, write a letter. Send a card. Say a prayer. Respond to a nudge with a simple act of love. God's purpose in this world and His plans for every person are powered by love.

FATHER, I WILL LISTEN CLOSELY AND ACT KINDLY TODAY, DOING EVERYTHING WITH LOVE.

FEBRUARY 12

May those who love the Lord
shine as the sun!
JUDGES 5:31

It takes more than sun to warm the earth,
And it's up to us to do it.
It's no good saying, "It'll be okay,"
If we don't help each other through it.
Love is a word that sounds nice
  when it's said,
But it truly needs more than a voice.
It needs a heartbeat, willing hands,
  and some feet—
Love stays alive with one's choice!

FATHER, I CHOOSE TO BE YOUR LOVE-
IN-ACTION TODAY. I THANK YOU IN
ADVANCE FOR LEADING THE WAY!

FEBRUARY 13

*This is how everyone will recognize
that you are My disciples—
when they see the love
you have for each other.*
JOHN 13:35 THE MESSAGE

Imagine hearing someone say, "I saw God today. He was in your kindness." Acts of love are beacons of light, streaming to earth from heaven. When we choose loving *actions* we start a chain *reaction* of good by reflecting the Giver of *everything* good. Being treated with love inspires more acts of love, and more acts of love in this world may change it for the better.

FATHER, BE IN MY CHOICES AND
ACTIONS TODAY, SO THAT THROUGH
ME, OTHERS GET A TASTE OF YOUR
LOVE

FEBRUARY 14

All we need is faith working through love.
GALATIANS 5:6

We have to believe love can change in us and in this world whatever doesn't reflect the nature of God, because love truly can and *will*. But love needs *you*—your heart, hands, feet, and faith. Love is a force set in motion by the One who created us and who transforms us by the power of His love. God loved us first...and when we love Him in return, He transforms into His likeness.

FATHER, LOVING YOU HAS CHANGED ME. IF AND WHEN OTHERS NOTICE, GIVE ME THE WORDS THAT GIVE YOU THE GLORY!

FEBRUARY 15

Whoever goes hunting for what is right and kind finds life itself—glorious life!
PROVERBS 21:21 THE MESSAGE

Loving God means being kind, helpful, patient, encouraging, and thoughtful. It means serving as Jesus Himself served. When we ask God's Spirit, He opens our eyes to the needs only He can see. When He does so, we have the chance to *do*— and by doing acts of love as God created us to do, we experience the *fullest* life. We truly feel alive when we serve.

FATHER, TODAY KEEP MY EYES OPEN AND MY HEART WILLING TO LOVE YOU BY SERVING OTHERS.

FEBRUARY 16

I've loved you the way my Father has loved me.
Make yourselves at home in my love.

JOHN 15:9 THE MESSAGE

Curl up in God's love and feel His warmth ease your weariness. Find yourself protected from the winds of worry and the pelting of the pain. Pull the comfort snuggly around you. Relax in the realness of Christ's love. It's here for what you hope for... near for what you need... faithful against what you fear. It *always* has your back for whatever that you face—and when you look back, you'll see its trace.

FATHER, THANK YOU FOR THE AMAZING, ABUNDANT, AND ALWAYS LOVE OF JESUS. LET IT OVERFLOW FROM MY LIFE TO OTHERS.

FEBRUARY 17

*God has given us the Holy Spirit
to fill our hearts with His love.*
ROMANS 5:5

When we completely open our heart to love, God will fill it. Then, when the frustrations of the day empty us of what love *is*—patience, kindness, generosity, selflessness, and forgiveness—we rely on God's power to enable us to be the people He wants us to be. Refilled with His love, we can choose to *pour it out on others*— and the more we share God's love, the more beautiful the world.

FATHER, I THANK YOU FOR YOUR LOVE:
IT IS THE FUEL THAT FILLS MY HEART
TODAY, ENABLING ME TO BE KIND AND
CARING.

FEBRUARY 18

Give thanks to the Lord, for He is good;
His love and His kindness go on forever.
I CHRONICLES 16:34

Love goes on and on into eternity as well as into our lives and through our hearts in a steady stream from the One who loves us faithfully and forever. Love emerges as big even in the little things. The simplicity of hope-filled words, a warm smile, or a *quiet listen*, for instance, can make a difference in any day—and with each moment like that, *we make a different world.*

FATHER, HELP ME NOTICE ALL THE LITTLE CHANCES I HAVE TO SHOW HOW BIG YOUR LOVE IS TODAY.

FEBRUARY 19

No matter what I say, what I believe,
and what I do, I'm bankrupt without love.
I CORINTHIANS 13:3 THE MESSAGE

Avoid overthinking, pausing, or blinking;
Let's love without question or quarrel.
Don't wait for good vibes, the right time,
   or a sign.
Don't look for ovations and laurel.
Without expectations or long hesitations,
Be brave toward whatever you've feared!
Love is in kindness and judgmental
   blindness.
By grace all offenses are cleared!

FATHER, YOUR COMMANDMENT IS TO
LOVE—YOU AND OTHERS—AND THEREBY
LIGHT THE WAY SO PEOPLE IN THE
DARK CAN SEE YOUR GRACE.

FEBRUARY 20

You didn't choose Me! I chose you!
I appointed you to go and
produce lovely fruit always.

JOHN 15:16

You are chosen! And the Creator of every part of your being knows that *every day* you can use the gifts He's given you. What you do *matters* no matter how un- or underappreciated you feel. Accolades don't make beautiful souls; God does. Let the work of your hands, from chore to charity, be an act of love for Him.

FATHER, HELP ME REMEMBER THAT YOU GAVE ME MY DAYS AND AS WELL AS MY GIFTEDNESS TO SERVE YOU.

FEBRUARY 21

Work for the good and don't quit.
PSALM 37:27 THE MESSAGE

There will be days when we feel like giving up on being nice and doing good. Feeling empty and dry, we might think it's our turn to sit back and soak up the kind of love and kindness we've sown. But consider that our reward actually comes with the *doing*, with the *giving. Love's reward is knowing that God is in the sowing*—so fill your day with acts of love and be confident that your heart is filling up too!

FATHER, MY STRENGTH AND JOY ARE IN YOU AND YOUR LOVE. I LOVE OTHERS FOR YOUR GLORY!

FEBRUARY 22

His compassion is intertwined
with everything He does.
PSALM 145:9

Choosing to put love into action weaves the grace and compassion of God into everything we do. This choice will bring on challenges, but God is our go-to strength. He will make us able to love intentionally and be kind consistently. He asks us to give to others what He freely gives to us—and that would be His grace. Every sunrise brings a new and needed portion of His grace.

FATHER, YOUR LOVE NEVER FAILS OR FALTERS. GIVE ME STRENGTH TO CHOOSE LOVING ACTIONS TODAY.

FEBRUARY 23

Live generously.
LUKE 6:30 THE MESSAGE

To live wholeheartedly, love big-heartedly!
Live each day pouring generous doses of
kindness into the world. Temper the quick,
impatient reactions with love. Go out of
your way to ask God to influence *all* your
ways! He—the Giver of abundant life—
makes the difference in a difficult world,
and He wants to *do so through you.*

FATHER, I WANT TO LIVE TO GIVE
GENEROUSLY. PLEASE POUR YOUR
LOVE AND GRACE INTO ALL I DO.

FEBRUARY 24

*We are able to hold our heads high no matter
what happens and know that all is well,
for we know how dearly God loves us.*
ROMANS 5:5

God dearly loves you, and He wants to
express His love *through* you to people
who are hurting or lonely or unaware of
God's love for them. Let your confidence
in God's love for you inspire you to share
His love with others. God's love changes
us and then challenges us to show His love
to the people He puts in our path.

FATHER, I DEPEND ON YOUR LOVE
TO EMPOWER ME TODAY, THAT I
MIGHT SHINE YOUR LIGHT INTO THE
DARKNESS OF PEOPLE'S LIVES.

FEBRUARY 25

Trust in the LORD, and do good.
PSALM 37:3 NKJV

Worries are weights that sap our energy. We can't do the good we want to do if we don't trust God with all that concerns us. Trust is letting go of everything— your desires, your discouragement, your wanting-to-give-up, and your wondering-when-the-storm-will-end. *All* this—*everything* about you—is on God's radar because you are *always* on His mind.

FATHER, I TRUST YOU. BY LETTING GO TODAY OF MY WORRIES AND FEARS, I CAN FREELY GIVE LOVE AND DO GOOD.

FEBRUARY 26

Help and give without expecting a return.
You'll never—I promise—regret it.
LUKE 6:35 THE MESSAGE

This truth that Jesus spoke is something to get excited about: He assures us that we'll *never* regret giving even behind the scenes...*because God sees and remembers.* Generous hearts hold something more valuable than all the riches in the world: a promise from the *eternally faithful* One who is powerful enough to bless us with more than we'll *ever* give away.

FATHER, USE MY LIFE AS AN OPEN
CHANNEL FOR YOUR LOVE AND
BLESSINGS TO FLOW THROUGH!

FEBRUARY 27

He knows us far better than we know ourselves... That's why we can be so sure that every detail in our lives of love for God is worked into something good.
ROMANS 8:27-28 THE MESSAGE

Perhaps He-who-made-me is just who
   I need.
I wonder..., Could love be the way
   to succeed?
It can't be that simple—or, then, *can* it be
That God works *all* into good things
   for me!

FATHER GOD, IT IS GOOD TO BE KNOWN AND LOVED BY YOU AND TO REST IN THE PROMISE THAT YOUR LOVE WORKS LIFE'S HARDEST TIMES INTO GOOD.

FEBRUARY 28

Grow in love for God and each other.
ACTS 14:22

By loving God *most*, we learn to love others *best*. When we give God first place in our lives, we shift our hearts into a giving mode. And when we are close to God, we realize how fully and freely we're loved *for no other reason than He wants to love us*. When we experience this unconditional love, the desire to offer that same kind of love to others begins to take root. That's how love grows: from God *to* us... to God *through* us.

FATHER, PLEASE CULTIVATE IN ME A FRESH SENSE OF YOUR LOVE SO I AM ABLE TO GENEROUSLY GIVE YOUR LOVE TO OTHERS.

MARCH 1

Nothing in all creation will ever be able to separate us from the love of God.
ROMANS 8:39 NLT

God's love has no limits and no conditions. It doesn't have strings attached, and we can't earn it by what we do or lose it because of what we don't do. We will never deserve His love. God is kind to *all*, generously. God loves *everyone*, equally. His love is a powerful life-changer in us and through us. Let's look for ways to be that power source today!

> FATHER, GIVE ME EYES TO SEE WHO NEEDS TO EXPERIENCE YOUR LOVE THROUGH ME TODAY.

MARCH 2

*You must love the L*ORD *your God
with all your heart, all your soul,
all your mind, and all your strength.*

MARK 12:30 NLT

Loving God most and putting Him first
in our lives is the only way to make *true*
love last in our lives. A relationship is simply a short-circuited system without Him.
When we welcome His perfect love into
our hearts, selfishness and skepticism get
pushed out, allowing the life-giving love
that every heart craves to flow freely from
God... through our lives... to others.

FATHER, I AM BLESSED BY YOUR
EXTRAVAGANT LOVE FOR ME. I ASK
YOU TO GIVE ME COURAGE TO SHOW
OTHERS THE SAME.

MARCH 3

We love Him because He first loved us.
1 JOHN 4:19 NKJV

God loved us before we loved Him, and we can't love others well without loving Him *back*. If we try to love people without God, then fear rooted in past pain, the flaws of being human, and the crippling pride that keeps us from receiving the transforming power of grace all get in the way. If we don't know God's love, we don't know how to love like He does—and He loves *best*.

FATHER, YOUR LOVE IS PERFECT AND POWERFUL. LET IT TRANSFORM ME DAILY SO THAT I CAN LOVE OTHERS WITH GRACE AND WISDOM.

MARCH 4

*Be kind to each other, tenderhearted,
forgiving one another, just as God through
Christ has forgiven you.*

EPHESIANS 4:32 NLT

We can never let love and kindness suc-
cumb to fear. If we fear people who look
different or think differently, we may stop
taking the initiative with love—*and when
we make that choice, we lose in every way.*
So love on! Show people the kindness you
yourself appreciate, keep a tender heart
toward others, and forgive quickly. Your
obedience glorifies God and makes the
world a better place.

FATHER, HELP MY HEART
STAY FREE OF FEAR AND BE FULL
OF KINDNESS TODAY.

MARCH 5

I want to show God's kindness.
II SAMUEL 9:3 NLT

One reason it feels good to be kind is because it feels good to be like our Father! Just as we don't earn God's love, our kindness and love should *never* have to be earned either. Kindness isn't a response to the way we're treated; being kind is our responsibility as a child of God. Oftentimes it simply takes a deep breath, a pause, and a smile to right our emotions and then do the right thing!

FATHER, GIVE ME PATIENCE AND STRENGTH TO SHOW OTHERS YOUR KINDNESS, FOR I KNOW THAT SIGHT BRINGS YOU JOY!

MARCH 6

Loving God includes loving people.
You've got to love both.
I JOHN 4:21 THE MESSAGE

Why are we on this planet if not to love? Without love, we go through the motions of living, missing the very thing that makes life most meaningful. People long to hear and *believe* this truth: *you are loved no matter what*. Knowing God's unconditional love and letting it light up the world through us is a privilege. Let's shine today by making every person feel a touch of His love!

FATHER, BY YOUR POWER AND PRESENCE, MAY I SPEAK AND ACT WITH YOUR LOVE TODAY.

MARCH 7

He is kind to the unthankful…
Be merciful, just as your Father
also is merciful.
LUKE 6:35-36 NKJV

Actions speak. Words have power. Smiles have a purpose! All can be expressions of love and kindness. *God is kind*; kindness is an aspect of His very nature. He doesn't decide whether or not to be kind. He is kind to everyone because He can't help it. Kindness is part of who God is; His tenderness is a testimony of His character. And *as He is*, we should want to be!

FATHER, HELP ME REFLECT YOUR KINDNESS TODAY ESPECIALLY TOWARD THOSE WHO NEED TO SEE IT MOST.

MARCH 8

*I lavish unfailing love
to a thousand generations.*
EXODUS 34:7 NLT

God's love for you is *overwhelming*...
over the moon, over the mistakes, over
the fears, over the faults, and over the
doubt. And God's love is as unfailing as it
is unfathomable. There isn't a thing in the
world you can do to weaken the love your
heavenly Father lavishes on you; the Love
that listens to you; the Love that is larger
than life's disappointments. Whatever today brings, know that God's love will bring
you through!

FATHER, YOUR LOVE IS MY STRENGTH
AND MY JOY. I'M THANKFUL IT NEVER
FAILS OR FALTERS.

MARCH 9

Conquer evil by doing good.
ROMANS 12:21

A loving heart does good things, chooses good words, and, as a result, shows others how incredibly good God's love is! Every day we get to share His love with those people who are right where we are, punctuating for them the power it holds. Love with an exclamation point today!

FATHER, MAKE MY HEART LIKE YOURS...
ABLE TO DO GOOD THINGS AND SPEAK
WITH LOVE.

MARCH 10

It's your heart, not the dictionary,
that gives meaning to your words.
A good person produces good deeds
and words season after season.
MATTHEW 12:34-35 THE MESSAGE

The only true *good* in us is *God* in us. When we realize how much we need God and we yield to Him, His love transforms our hearts. Being able to do good things *season after season* requires our surrender to the Savior. Jesus' sacrificial death on the cross provides us a bridge from our *selfishness* to love's *selflessness*—and God's goodness can get into the world through His selfless people.

FATHER, I SURRENDER TO YOU SO THAT I AM ABLE—IN YOUR POWER—TO BRING GENUINE LOVE AND GOODNESS TO OTHERS.

MARCH 11

*Let your good deeds glow for all to see,
so that they will praise your heavenly Father.*

MATTHEW 5:16

The way to glow is to believe, to *know*,
And our Father in heaven is the One
  who'll show!
When we're good to others, when
  we put love first,
When we quench the world's *deepest*
  thirst.
His love has a glimmer, a shimmer,
  a shine...
That pierces the darkness with the good
  and the kind.
So let's be a beam, a gleam, or a stream,
Of God's light and love, so His heart can
  be seen.

FATHER, HELP ME GLOW WITH YOUR
GOODNESS AND LIGHT UP MY CORNER
OF THE WORLD WITH YOUR LOVE!

MARCH 12

*Demonstrate the love
and kindness of the Lord.*
I SAMUEL 20:14

Every day we're given opportunities to paint a clearer picture of God's love with our words and, more important, our *ways*. Love expressed in deed is often more powerful than love exclaimed in words! The speech can be heard, but the actions can change a heart. So don't hesitate to *do* love today. Be moved to *move*...with kindness, consideration, and compassion.

FATHER, LET YOUR LOVE BE IN WHAT I DO, NOT JUST IN WHAT I SAY.

MARCH 13

You are a God of forgiveness,
always ready to pardon,
gracious and merciful,
slow to become angry, and full of love.
NEHEMIAH 9:17

Can we imagine being *always ready* to forgive? *Always* means not a moment spent dwelling on the wrongdoing or the hurt. Not a second sacrificed to sulking. Rather, we choose to respond to an offense with the *fullness of love*. That's God's way. With enough practice, we'll get better and better at it—and the world will become better and better too!

FATHER, FILL MY HEART WITH YOUR LOVE SO THAT I AM ALWAYS READY TO FORGIVE.

MARCH 14

No mind has imagined
what God has prepared
for those who love Him.
I CORINTHIANS 2:9 NLT

Keep it up! Keep loving God with all your heart. Keep loving others. Keep being kind. Keep exercising compassion. Keep offering help. Keep etching the signature of Christ on the lives of others with the eternal ink of love that will never fade. Keep loving God by putting more of His love in the world...all the while knowing that He is preparing *unimaginably* good things for those people who, like you, love Him!

FATHER, BY LOVING YOU, I LEARN TO LOVE OTHERS. BY BEING LOVED BY YOU, I LEARN TO LOVE OTHERS. I THANK YOU FOR YOUR LOVE.

MARCH 15

His love and His kindness go on forever.
I CHRONICLES 16:34

Like waves to the shore, God's love for you
and His kindness to you are ceaseless and
certain. He's not giving up on you... *ever*.
How different the world would be if we
were as relentless about sharing His love
and being kind! Rather than changing the
world, work on making today brighter by
choosing once again to be God's hands...
His feet... His heart. And do the same
tomorrow... and the day after that... and
the day after that.... You get the idea.

FATHER, TEACH ME TO SHARE YOUR
LOVE AND KINDNESS FAITHFULLY AND
WITH COMPASSION.

MARCH 16

Even before He made the world,
God chose us to be His very own.
EPHESIANS 1:4

Live today knowing you were chosen *before* you lived a day! You are God's very own. As children created by perfect Love, we have been chosen and called to live a life of love. When we love others, we reflect the One who loved us *first* and we are doing what He asked us to do *most*.

FATHER, LEAD MY HEART BY YOUR
PERFECT LOVE AND LET MY ACTIONS
FOLLOW YOUR EXAMPLE OF SELFLESS,
GENEROUS LOVE.

MARCH 17

Discover beauty in everyone.
ROMANS 12:17 THE MESSAGE

Love is the means by which we recognize the beauty of a soul. Love is the heart-seeking force that breaks down walls and brings light to dark places. When life is hard and suffering is long, we can lose sight of our intrinsic and infinite value to God. His love—received through His people—reminds us. Let's extend that kind of remembering love today as we recognize the beauty of every soul who crosses our path.

FATHER, HELP ME LIVE WITH YOUR EYES OF LOVE TODAY. ENABLE ME TO SEE THE GENUINE BEAUTY OF EVERY PERSON YOU CREATED AND LOVE.

MARCH 18

Through Christ, all the kindness of God
has been poured out upon us.

ROMANS 1:5

Kindness and love go hand in- hand. In
fact, some of love's sweetest qualities are
evident in our kind actions and reactions.
Also, since Jesus is the ultimate way God
poured out His kindness, our kindness
can be considered an embodiment of His
great love. And if we've accepted and now
stand in God's grace evident in Christ's
sacrificial death for our sins, may we cooperate with God as He uses us to keep
kindness flowing into the world and love
streaming through it to change it.

FATHER, USE ME TODAY TO SHARE
YOUR KINDNESS AND YOUR LOVE IN A
WORLD HUNGRY FOR BOTH.

MARCH 19

*Everything got started in Him
and finds its purpose in Him.*
COLOSSIANS 1:16 THE MESSAGE

Like everything else, love begins with God. And a truly God-centered, God-seeking life will stay surrendered to the good of others and committed to the giving of grace. Love is *never* selfish—and that's an order too tall for us in our humanness. *We need God's help* if love stands a chance of getting through us and into the world. Let's make today a love giveaway by giving our waking hours to God before we begin!

FATHER, I SURRENDER MY HEART TO YOU TODAY: LET YOUR LOVE HAVE ITS WAY IN ME AND THROUGH ME.

MARCH 20

He'll calm you with His love.
ZEPHANIAH 3:17 THE MESSAGE

Schedules demand, time flies, and quiet eludes. Invite God to bring the calm. *Is calmness even possible?* Only with His love—a love that, when we welcome it and surrender to it, makes it *impossible* for us to be fearful, frazzled, or fed up. When stress presses in, take a second to breathe deeply, say Jesus' name, and know love's calming effect. Doing so has a beautiful way of connecting us to our Lord so our actions reveal Him to others.

FATHER, WHEN I RUN OUT OF PATIENCE, LET ME RUN TO YOU AND KNOW THE STRENGTH OF YOUR LOVE.

MARCH 21

When the Holy Spirit controls our lives
He will produce this kind of fruit in us:
love, joy, peace, patience, kindness,
goodness, faithfulness,
gentleness and self-control.
GALATIANS 5:22-23

Oh, *Control.* How we try to hold onto you with all we've got. Then, when circumstances shake our hands loose again, we let go. We have been reminded that our hearts, minds, and spirits are best off when God is in control and *He* is producing fruit in our lives that blesses others. Let's pray for lack of control and leave everything to God today. *Love will grow wild!*

FATHER, GIVE ME THE HUMILITY
AND GRACE TO SURRENDER
EVERYTHING TO YOU.

MARCH 22

Love is very patient and kind.
I CORINTHIANS 13:4

Patience is hard—and it's tested on many levels on many days. But love puts the *very* before patient and kind. When we can't squeeze out another ounce of grace for whatever or *whomever* is in front of us, love emphasizes the godly—the patient and kind—response. We can do for others what God does for us: Be *very* patient. Be *very* kind. Be *love*.

FATHER, THANK YOU FOR YOUR LOVE
THAT IS ALWAYS PATIENT AND KIND.
HELP ME LOVE THAT WAY TOO.

MARCH 23

*May your roots go down deep
into the soil of God's marvelous love.*
EPHESIANS 3:17

God's love is our life source. It fuels our growth into His likeness and produces beautiful fruit in our lives. It's up to us to send our spiritual roots deep into His love *every day* so they are nourished and strengthened, not easily pulled out by anger, impatience, or fear. The deeper we're rooted in God's love, the more freely we'll be able to love others and bless them.

FATHER, LET MY SPIRIT STAY
DEPENDENT ON YOUR LOVE
SO I CAN FREELY SHARE YOUR LOVE
WITH OTHERS.

MARCH 24

*Christ became a human being and lived here
on earth among us and was full of loving
forgiveness and truth.*

JOHN 1:14

When Jesus walked in our shoes, He was
"full of loving forgiveness and truth." Now
His Spirit is at home in our hearts, filling us
with the same good stuff if we empty ourselves of *ourselves* to receive it. Respond-
ing with love means turning on Jesus to
start the day and lead the way!

FATHER, FILL ME TO OVERFLOWING
WITH YOUR LOVE AND
MAY IT GUIDE MY WORDS
AS I SHARE YOUR GOSPEL TRUTH.

MARCH 25

Pursue a righteous life—a life of wonder,
faith, love, steadiness, courtesy.
I TIMOTHY 6:11 THE MESSAGE

Today, let's pursue the life God designed us to live! May our acts of kindness touch hearts and inspire a deep appreciation of our Creator. Let's be thoughtful in ordinary moments of everyday routines when it's not expected, but it *is* exactly what's needed. When we shatter the mundane with the love of the Most High, we are most alive—because in those moments we are *most like Him*.

FATHER, I WANT TO LOVE WITH YOUR
LOVE IN MOMENTS ONLY YOU SEE...
TO THOSE WHO MATTER MOST TO ME.

MARCH 26

*Happy are those who long
to be just and good.*
MATTHEW 5:6

Happiness comes as we seek after God. Put differently, living happily happens when we long to be where we belong—*in Him*—doing exactly what He created us to do: *love*! Love is always just and good, and God's love is all that we need to change the world as His *love changes us*. The more we give, the more we grow—and the more we glow!

FATHER, I'M HAPPIEST WHEN I'M CLOSEST TO YOU, LONGING TO BE MORE LIKE YOU.

MARCH 27

*He has told us from the very first
to love each other.*
II JOHN 1:6

Since God says, "Do this: *love*,"
Maybe all else falls into place.
Love others for one good reason,
  one great thing—
It's how the world will glimpse Him
  face-to-face.

FATHER, FILL ME WITH YOUR SPIRIT
TODAY, SO THAT MY HEART'S
OVERFLOW WILL BE NOTHING OTHER
THAN YOUR LOVE, GRACE,
AND KINDNESS.

MARCH 28

*All praise to God
for His wonderful kindness to us.*
EPHESIANS 1:6

I love the fact that God is *kind*. His love is not only strong and tough; His love is also kind. Kindness is evident in the tender touch of a word or a fulfilled desire that no one but God could know about. He is always incredibly kind to us because of His all-consuming love for us—and we should *always* respond with gratitude for the wonderful ways He shows it.

FATHER, THANK YOU FOR BEING KIND IN THE MOST PERSONAL AND MEANINGFUL WAYS. I DO LOVE YOU WITH ALL I AM.

MARCH 29

Love forgets mistakes.
PROVERBS 17:9

Love is forgetful. It forgets the messes we make with our words and actions, with our finger-pointing and false accusations. God forgives and then forgets *every time we fall*—because love uses grace to erase. If we're going to love well, we'll learn to forget well how badly and how often we blow it...And we'll be able to forget well as we remember how deep the well of God's forgiving love for you.

FATHER, GIVE ME GRACE TO OFFER GRACE TO OTHERS, THROUGH THE POWER OF YOUR LOVE.

MARCH 30

*It is good when you truly obey
our Lord's command,
"You must love and help your neighbors."*
JAMES 2:8

Let's ask God to open our eyes to a neighbor's need... to guide our prayers to a friend's hurting heart... to send us to sit with someone and listen without saying a word. Love sometimes is simply the gift of *time*. Our dizzyingly full days can have us rushing past important things, yet love will always be *the most important thing*—and today will offer you countless ways to share it!

> FATHER, HELP ME SLOW DOWN SO
> I DON'T MISS OPPORTUNITIES TO
> LISTEN, PRAY, AND SERVE FROM A
> HEART OF LOVE.

MARCH 31

Tell the world about His wondrous love.
ISAIAH 12:4

Selflessness is how we show the world about love. Selflessness is evident when we are kind, when we are thoughtful, and when we put the needs of others before our own. Love *values* others, saying with words and actions, "You are priceless. You have purpose. You are irreplaceable." Let's shout those affirmations with our actions today! Let's get loud for love and magnify God in all we do.

FATHER, PLEASE ENABLE ME
TO TELL THE WORLD ABOUT
YOUR LOVE THROUGH MY ACTIONS
AS WELL AS MY WORDS.

APRIL 1

*How well He understands us
and knows what is best for us at all times.*
EPHESIANS 1:8

It's a gift to be understood and loved, to be allowed the freedom to be who God created us to be. It's a gift to be loved without conditions or judgments. If we love like this—which is how God loves us—and if we love no matter what, we reflect God's love. May His unconditional love *through* us bless everyone He brings into our lives.

FATHER, GIVE ME YOUR HEART FOR OTHERS. HELP ME UNDERSTAND THEM, RECOGNIZE THEIR NEEDS, AND RESPOND WITH YOUR LOVE.

APRIL 2

The godly love to give!
PROVERBS 21:26

Love gives and *loves* to give.
It's how a life should love to live!
And at the heart of beating hearts,
Love is how the healing starts.

FATHER, PLEASE GIVE ME A HEART
THAT LOVES TO GIVE. GRACE, LOVE,
HOPE, ENCOURAGEMENT, TIME,
RESOURCES—WHATEVER YOU ASK OF
ME, LET MY ANSWER BE "YES, FATHER!
ANYTHING FOR YOU."

APRIL 3

Let love guide your life.
COLOSSIANS 3:14

Today let's not be pulled along by the pressures of this world, but instead be guided
by God's grace and love! We're going to
let love lead the way, helping us choose
our words and know how to act. We're going to slow down on the emotional front
and instead use our spiritual fortitude—
for God's Spirit in us always, *always* draws
from and delivers *love*.

> FATHER, LET ME BE GUIDED BY YOUR
> LOVE ALONE TODAY. I AM READY TO BE
> LED BY YOUR SPIRIT.

APRIL 4

My God is changeless in His love for me.
PSALM 59:10

Ah, God's *changeless* love... He never withdraws it because of our weakness or willfulness, and it is never diminished even when we fail to love others. He loves us *completely*, and He'll *never* change His mind about it! How can we be so saturated with God's love and not share it with every soul that crosses our path? We can! Let's soak the world around us in God's love today—and flood our Father's heart with joy.

FATHER, THANK YOU FOR
YOUR CONSTANT LOVE. LET IT FLOW
THROUGH ME TO THE HEARTS
OF OTHERS.

APRIL 5

May you be able to feel and understand,
as all God's children should, how long,
how wide, how deep, and
how high His love really is.
EPHESIANS 3:18

God wants you to feel loved today! And
He wants you to understand that you
don't have to do a *thing* to earn His love.
You don't have to get everything right or
pay for your wrongs. You don't have to do
more, be more, or give more. He's the One
who's all about *more*—but more compassion, more grace, more hope, and more
love for you than you'll *ever* comprehend.

> FATHER, I'M THANKFUL FOR YOUR
> FAITHFUL, FATHOMLESS LOVE—
> AND FOR THE JOY I FIND IN GIVING IT
> TO OTHERS!

APRIL 6

*Long before He laid down earth's foundations,
He had us in mind, had settled on us as the
focus of His love, to be made whole
and holy by His love.*
EPHESIANS 1:4 THE MESSAGE

God's love makes us whole—because He heals us and gives us purpose—and holy—because He sets us apart from the world to be in relationship with Him and to love others with His love. *We can't truly love without Him*, but with Him, any encouraging word, act of kindness, or heartfelt prayer will be love-drenched and God-glorifying.

FATHER, I WANT SHOWING YOUR LOVE
AND SHARING IT TO BE MY DEEPEST
DESIRE TODAY.

APRIL 7

Love from the center of who you are;
don't fake it.
ROMANS 12:10 THE MESSAGE

If we're going to love others free of conditions and expectations and if we are going to love when we don't feel like it, then we have to learn to be completely dependent on God. After all, His is the authentic love that *chose* us and *transformed* us. Love isn't always the immediate response of our flesh, but when our spirits stay in tune with and surrendered to God, He will fill us with His love that will always be victorious over the response of our flesh.

FATHER, I SURRENDER MY SPIRIT TO
YOU AND TRUST YOUR LOVE TO GUIDE
ME IN ALL I DO.

APRIL 8

*Show me Your strong love
in wonderful ways.*
PSALM 17:7

God's love is strong. When it comes to healing a heart or lifting a soul, *only* His compassionate love has the necessary strength. God's love makes its way into places of our human struggle that we don't always talk about, and His love has the power to heal and mend. Of course God's love is a perfect match: He Himself designed us to *need* it. We'll have so many chances to meet that need for other people today. Let's do exactly that. Let's go out and love!

FATHER, YOUR LOVE IS STRONG AND WONDERFUL. LET ME BE FAITHFUL TO SHARE IT WITH OTHERS.

APRIL 9

Be gentle with one another, sensitive.
EPHESIANS 4:32 THE MESSAGE

The pressure and pull of our daily lives can put a strain on our ability to be gentle and sensitive. Those traits can be the first to go from our love storehouse, easily stolen by our impatience, short tempers, and the cares we insist on carrying. But we *can* be gentle and thoughtful when we choose to be God-centered and thankful. At the start of the day, let's pray that *love* guides our way!

FATHER, HELP ME LIVE WITH GOD-CENTERED GRATITUDE TODAY SO THAT I CAN BE GENTLE AND THOUGHTFUL, IN WORD AND IN DEED.

APRIL 10

Keep your eyes open, hold tight to your convictions, give it all you've got, be resolute, and love without stopping.
I CORINTHIANS 16:13-14 THE MESSAGE

Let's love nonstop today! Let's be determined to love even those who are hard to love.. After all, *sharing God's love is simply what matters most in life.* And sharing God's love should guide us when we choose our words and interact with others. We are to be living reflections of our loving God. May we give it all we've got!

FATHER, USE ME TO REFLECT YOUR LOVE TODAY.

APRIL 11

Don't seek vengeance. Don't bear a grudge;
but love your neighbor as yourself.

LEVITICUS 19:18

Hurt feelings are hard on the heart, and holding on to them weighs us down and suffocates our ability to love. Our hearts aren't designed to store the ledgers of all the ways we've been offended and hurt. When we let go—and God will help us— we are freer to wholeheartedly love others. It's what He wants us to do every day, without letting a fragment of bitterness stand in the way.

FATHER, I GIVE TO YOU ALL THE CLUTTER IN MY HEART AND MY MIND SO THAT I CAN LOVE OTHERS FULLY, FEARLESSLY, AND FREELY!

APRIL 12

No one has ever seen God.
But if we love each other, God lives in us,
and His love is brought to
full expression in us.
I JOHN 4:12 NLT

We can show the world a "full expression" of God's love by *loving each other*. What an amazing truth! When we choose to treat a person kindly, give sacrificially to someone who has less than we do, or serve at the homeless shelter, we are loving with Christlike love.. After we walk away—and by God's grace—His love may change a life.

FATHER, LET YOUR LOVE COME TO
FULL EXPRESSION IN MY WORDS AND
ACTIONS TODAY.

APRIL 13

*God is working in you, giving you the desire
and the power to do what pleases Him.*
PHILIPPIANS 2:13 NLT

God is at work in us at all times, enabling us to please Him in all we say and do. Remembering that we belong to Him and that His Spirit lives within us, we will be more motivated and empowered to do kind, loving things. As a result, we succeed at the *greatest* thing: we live *a life that pleases Him*.

FATHER, I WANT TO DO WHAT PLEASES
YOU TODAY WITH A HUMBLE AND
SURRENDERED HEART.

APRIL 14

*Even if I had the gift of faith so that I could
speak to a mountain and make it move,
I would still be worth nothing at all
without love.*

I CORINTHIANS 13:2

Mountain-moving faith doesn't compare
to the power of love that is able to move
hearts to recognize the grace and goodness of God. His love is incredibly strong
and remarkably kind. Sharing God's love
is the very reason we came to be, and His
love is the only thing we truly need. And
here we are, with opportunities to offer
God's love to *everyone* in our lives and
anyone He brings across our path.

FATHER, LOVE IS THE MOST IMPORTANT
GIFT YOU GIVE. PLEASE GIVE IT
GENEROUSLY TO OTHERS
THROUGH ME TODAY.

APRIL 15

I never lose sight of Your love,
but keep in step with You,
never missing a beat.
PSALM 26:3 THE MESSAGE

Never losing sight of God's love enables us to never miss a chance to love others. We will be blessed, for instance, when we look and love *outward*, when we meet needs, offer kindness, and show compassion. As we do these things, as we draw from the well of God's love within us, He fills us with more of not only His love but also His joy, strength, courage, peace, and hope—everything our hearts need *most*.

FATHER, FILL MY HEART WITH YOUR
GOODNESS SO THE OVERFLOW WILL
BE A SELFLESS AND JOYFUL LOVE
FOR OTHERS.

APRIL 16

There is no god like You in heaven or earth,
for You are loving and kind and
You keep Your promises.

I KINGS 8:23

There are so many ways to love, and if we pay attention, we'll see that God reveals how it's done. His kindness is evident in a beautiful sunrise; His thoughtfulness, in a needed rain shower; and His encouragement, in a heartfelt desire quietly fulfilled. We can also love by using the gifts He gave us to be kind, thoughtful, and encouraging. God can work through us to scatter love how and when it's needed most.

FATHER, LEAD ME BY YOUR SPIRIT
TODAY, AND USE ME TO REVEAL YOUR
LOVE IN WONDERFUL WAYS.

APRIL 17

*Love never gives up, never loses faith,
is always hopeful, and endures
through every circumstance.*

I CORINTHIANS 13:7 NLT

Today is a good day for *never-give-up* love! When things don't go exactly right (they probably won't), when our patience gets tested (it probably will be), and when God allows some faith-building opportunities (He usually does), let's keep loving. Our choice to love others with God's love has a calming effect on us and on everyone around us—and God's love as close as a deep breath, a prayer pause, and our gratitude for grace.

FATHER, I'LL LOOK TO YOU FOR ALL
I NEED TO BE ABLE TO LOVE WITH
NEVER-GIVE-UP LOVE.

APRIL 18

Love us, GOD, with all You've got—
that's what we're depending on.
PSALM 33:22 THE MESSAGE

Our hearts were created to love. It's what we need to *give* and to *get* throughout our life journey. Not a single soul is exempt from the pain and trials of life, and when we love each other along the way by extending a hand and helping one another up when we stumble, we follow God's lead, share His love, and glorify Him.

FATHER, I DEPEND ON YOUR LOVE
TO WORK IN ME AND THROUGH ME
SO I CAN BE A LIGHT OF YOUR LOVE
TO OTHERS.

APRIL 19

Fill all who love You with Your happiness.
PSALM 5:11

Feeling loved makes us happy; knowing we're loved completely, unconditionally, and infinitely fills us with indescribable joy! And that kind of complete, unconditional, infinite love has only one Source: God. We should want *everyone* to know the love of God and the joy that accompanies it. He chose us to be the messengers, the vessels, and the *reflection* of His love, and it can shine through the simplest act of kindness today!

FATHER, OPEN MY EYES AND MY HEART TO EVERY CHANCE I HAVE TO REFLECT YOUR LOVE TODAY!

APRIL 20

I will tell of the loving-kindnesses of God.
I will praise Him for all He has done.
ISAIAH 63:7

You can say it without sound
And turn this whole wide world around.
You can put it into words,
The nicest sentence ever heard!
You can show it when you smile
Or sit and listen for a while.
It shines brightly when you're kind,
The greatest gift you'll give (or *find*).
Love is not one thing, you see.
So spread some love creatively!

FATHER, SHOW ME HOW AND
WHERE TO SCATTER SEEDS
OF YOUR LOVE TODAY!

APRIL 21

The love of the LORD remains forever with those who fear Him.

PSALM 103:17 NLT

Be the reason someone sees the forever-love of our faithful God today! You can do that with something as simple as a smile or as monumental as meeting a significant need by doing something you've had on your heart to do for someone... who—you later learn—has been quietly praying for God to take care of that task. God leads by heartfelt nudges, the often small urges that don't go away. If He asks, it will mean a great deal here—and make an even greater difference in eternity.

FATHER, LET ME FOLLOW YOUR SPIRIT AND EXPRESS YOUR LOVE WHERE AND HOW YOU CHOOSE.

APRIL 22

Cheerful givers are the ones God prizes.
II CORINTHIANS 9:7

Giving is such a beautiful reflection of God, no wonder it spreads such joy! Giving is love in action, and God calls—He commands—us to love. So write that note, make a call, open a door, tip generously— look for ways to give, and God will give you ways to do it!

FATHER, MY HEART AND MY HANDS ARE OPEN. PLEASE SHOW ME WAYS TO GIVE FROM THE INFINITE WELLSPRING OF YOUR LOVE.

APRIL 23

*Pour out Your unfailing love
on those who know You!*
PSALM 36:10

We're *drenched* in God's perfect love! May we therefore empty the overflow into the lives of *everyone* our lives touch. It's not easy on days when we're hurting, hurried, or feeling helpless—*but God's love brings hope*. When we lack the strength to give, He steps in to love us back to hearts that are full, fearless, and ready to pour into others from the One whose love *never fails*.

FATHER, FILL ME WITH YOUR LOVE AND STRENGTH SO THAT I CAN LOVE WITH GRACE AND COURAGE.

APRIL 24

Love prospers when a fault is forgiven.
PROVERBS 17:9 NLT

Love prevails when we forgive. When we hold on to a hurt, we hurt only ourselves. Love does not stay stuck on whose fault, a focus that stops the flow of God's goodness in our lives. But when we focus on the forgiveness we both need and receive from Him, we see a clearer path to extend forgiveness to others. Forgive quickly, let love grow wildly, and watch your life become a field of beauty and blessing!

FATHER, CREATE IN ME A HEART THAT FORGIVES FREELY SO THAT YOUR LOVE WILL PREVAIL IN MY LIFE.

APRIL 25

I am with you; that is all you need.

II CORINTHIANS 12:9

We have all we need to bring God's love to the world... because we have *Him*! He's steady when our emotions aren't; He's patient when our patience is gone; and He sees the aching heart when all we see is the person in front of us. *And maybe in the moment that person is hard to love.* If that's the case, may we remember that God is *all we need* to respond to their love-need...and His will is that we *always* do so.

FATHER, REMIND ME TODAY THAT YOU ARE ALL I NEED TO OFFER E LOVE THAT OTHERS NEED.

APRIL 26

Give yourselves to the gifts God gives you.
I CORINTHIANS 14:1 THE MESSAGE

Your expression of love is as unique as your God-given gifts, and He will lead you to love others using those special qualities. After all, love is one purpose that God created and gifted *all* of us to fulfill! God will direct your path to those who need to see His love through *you*. Whether your steps take you through the rooms of your home, the hallways of an office, or around the world, know you're there to *love*!

FATHER, THANK YOU FOR GIVING ME
UNIQUE WAYS TO EXPRESS
YOUR LOVE. HELP ME BE FAITHFUL
TO USE THEM.

APRIL 27

How precious is Your constant love, O God!

PSALM 36:7

We all have those days when we feel unworthy, those days that find us moody and messy and more focused on our circumstances than on the *constant love* of our Creator. But no matter how we feel, the truth remains: we are *incredibly* loved. Infinitely, invincibly, *irrefutably* loved—for all our days on earth and for all eternity. And it's OK to simply *rest* in that truth today.

FATHER, YOU LOVE ME CONSTANTLY
AND UNCONDITIONALLY.
YOUR FAITHFULNESS IS MY REFUGE
AND MY HOPE.

APRIL 28

God loves you very much.
DANIEL 9:23

God's love is *much more*—more than the mistakes we made yesterday, more than the way we feel today, more than the way others make us feel from time to time. And thankfully there is nothing we can do to make Him love us more or less. Right this moment you are loved more than you can imagine. Look at the cross if you have any doubts. Then let that truth of God's love for you sink in. You are more than prepared to let it shine out into a world that needs love more than *anything* else.

FATHER, YOUR LOVE FOR ME CAN'T BE
SHAKEN OR SHATTERED,
SO PLEASE HELP ME SHARE IT
MORE FREELY THAN EVER.

APRIL 29

*Let everything you do reflect
your love of the truth.*

TITUS 2:7

There's no greater truth than this: Jesus gave His life for *every* life—for the hurt and the afraid, for the hopeless and the skeptical, for the disheartened believer and the unbeliever. We'll be challenged to love these souls along our journey, knowing because we know their Creator that none is unlovable. God's desire is for *all* to see, however brief the glimpse, evidence of the love of the One who gave His life to save them.

FATHER, PLEASE HELP ME BE A CLEAR EXPRESSION OF YOUR LOVE BY SHARING THE GOSPEL OF JESUS' DEATH AND RESURRECTION, THE ULTIMATE ACT OF LOVE.

APRIL 30

My God is changeless in His love for me.
PSALM 59:10

God is never going to change His mind about loving you. On your worst day, when every nerve is frazzled, your words aren't kind, guilt weighs heavily, and circumstances bully your worth, know this: not one bit of God's infinite love for you has fallen to the ground. His love is not based on your performance or your feelings or your sense of whether or not you merit it. God loves because He *is* love, and that truth is changeless.

FATHER, THANK YOU FOR LOVING ME WITHOUT CONDITION. HELP ME TO NEVER GIVE UP ON SHARING YOUR LOVE WITH OTHERS.

MAY 1

*Your love for one another will prove to the
world that you are My disciples.*
JOHN 13:35 NLT

When it comes to loving others, we don't
need to think outside the box; we simply
need to think outside *ourselves*. The need
is everywhere, in everyone around us. God
has put the order in things...the lives we
come in contact with, the people who
cross our path, the family and friends who
make up our inner circle. They're in place
for a reason—and we're in place for a reason. And the reason is love.

FATHER, MY LOVE FOR OTHERS IS THE
BEST REFLECTION OF YOU. I ASK YOU
TO CONTINUE TO MAKE ME A CLEARER
AND MORE WINSOME ONE.

MAY 2

Make yourselves at home in My love.
JOHN 15:9 THE MESSAGE

God's love is where we're fully forgiven and forever home. His love is the place where grace is found, where we realize that what we have—the love and forgiveness we've been *freely* given—is what *every person needs*. God gives us the privilege of sharing His love in countless ways throughout our day. May we never ignore the stirring in our heart to do even the smallest act of kindness. Our all-knowing *God* will direct us to where it will make the greatest impact.

FATHER, GIVE ME THE COURAGE AND CONFIDENCE TO LOVE WHERE YOU LEAD TODAY.

MAY 3

May you be given more and more
of God's kindness, peace, and love.
JUDE 1:2

The more love and kindness we pour
out, the more God pours *in*! He gives us
the good stuff in abundant measure, and
He chose us for the special assignment
of filling the earth with it. His love can
be revealed in endless ways, often quiet
and simple ways. Also, since every soul is
priceless to Him, *every* act of kindness is
invaluable. God may use it to turn a heart
toward Him.

FATHER, FILL ME WITH YOUR LOVE AND
LET IT POUR FORTH FROM MY LIFE,
POINTING PEOPLE TO YOU.

MAY 4

We know that all things work together
for good to those who love God,
to those who are the called
according to His purpose.
ROMANS 8:28 NKJV

I love You, Father. That simple declaration of love is the best way to start *any* day. As we look to God with those words, we receive the strength and desire to love others *better*. We can't do it without Him. He's the Source of kindness, forgiveness, and patience, of all aspects of love. So may we who have been "called according to His purpose" love others with His love.

FATHER, THANK YOU FOR GIVING ME
THE BEAUTIFUL PURPOSE OF SHOWING
YOUR LOVE TO OTHERS.

MAY 5

*Whatever is good and perfect is a gift
coming down to us from God our Father.*
JAMES 1:17 NLT

God's love is perfect. And every good
thing that comes into or flows out of our
lives finds its source in that love. God's
love has transformed our hearts, and when
we name Jesus our Savior and Lord, God's
love shapes our lives. Everything that
God allows us to experience, every storm
we go through, grows our trust in our
all-loving God.

FATHER, I KNOW THE GIFT OF YOUR
LOVE IS FOR EVERYONE. HELP ME
GRACIOUSLY AND GENEROUSLY GIVE
IT TO OTHERS TODAY.

MAY 6

Act with love...
and always depend on Him.
HOSEA 12:6 NLT

When we choose to act with love, we give the world a glimpse of God. He's right there, in every kind thing we do. No one else—nothing else—gets the credit. If an action is good, caring, loving, and generous, it's because of *Him*! We're an understudy in this life of love: He loved us first. He calls us to follow His example, but He doesn't stop there. He also assures us that we can't count on Him to help us love.

FATHER, I AM GRATEFUL FOR PEOPLE IN MY LIFE WHO HAVE LOVED ME WITH YOUR LOVE. PLEASE USE ME TODAY TO LOVE PEOPLE WHO NEED YOUR LOVE— AND THAT'S PRETTY MUCH EVERYONE. I'M DEPENDING ON YOU TO HELP ME!

MAY 7

Help and give without expecting a return.
You'll never—I promise—regret it.
LUKE 6:35 THE MESSAGE

Love and let go! The temptation to wait for a thank you or to expect something in return for a kindness can keep us from freely loving others the way God loves *us*. His love is without measure, free of strings, and freely given—and may our sharing of His love be like that too! If we develop the lifestyle of being kind, generous, and helpful without looking for an earthly or human reward, God will move us forward into the greater blessings of even more opportunities to give!

FATHER, GIVE ME A HEART LIKE
YOURS THAT GIVES GENEROUSLY,
WITHOUT MEASURE OR CONDITION OR
EXPECTATION.

MAY 8

Let your good deeds
shine out for all to see,
so that everyone will praise
your heavenly Father.
MATTHEW 5:16 NLT

Kindness *beams.* When our actions reflect
our heavenly Father, they stream His light
into a dark world, into hearts hungry for
His love. Directing people's attention to
Him is the greatest reward of any good
deed we do! Acts of love and kindness
can indeed lead people toward the arms
of God. All we do apart from Him will fade;
all we do for Him will shine forever.

FATHER, LET ME SHARE YOUR KINDNESS
WITH SOMEONE TODAY AND PLEASE
USE THAT ACT TO TURN THEIR HEART
TOWARD YOU.

MAY 9

*Speak the truth in love, growing in every way
more and more like Christ.*

EPHESIANS 4:15 NLT

We become "more and more like Christ"
when we *practice* being like Him—and
there's no better way to be like Jesus
than to be kind and to love well. Our
greatest growth toward Christlikeness,
however, can come in the hardest circumstances, when we don't know what God
is doing but we pray, "Thy will be done";
when we're drained of our strength and
forced to rely His. In those times we realize our weakness brings a wealth of
His presence—and when He's present,
love flourishes!

FATHER, HELP ME TO "SPEAK THE
TRUTH IN LOVE" JUST AS JESUS DID.
HELP ME TO BECOME MORE LIKE HIM IN
EVERY OTHER WAY AS WELL.

MAY 10

We prove ourselves by our purity,
our understanding, our patience,
our kindness, by the Holy Spirit within us,
and by our sincere love.
II CORINTHIANS 6:6 NLT

Love can be effectively—even powerful-ly—communicated without words. When we love someone, for instance, with our patience, kindness, helping hands, sacri-ficed time, or giving despite our own pain, the presence of God within us is revealed. We don't love so that we're seen; we love so the world *sees Him.* And the world sees Him clearly and He is glorified when we share His love with others.

FATHER, MY DESIRE IS TO LOVE WITH A PURE AND SINCERE HEART, SO THAT MY ACTIONS REVEAL YOU.

MAY 11

Live in such a way that
you are a credit to the Message of Christ.
PHILIPPIANS 1:27 THE MESSAGE

Our lives are love projectors. What is the world seeing on the screen of your life? Ideally we are living out forgiveness, a kind demeanor, a gentle attitude, compassion, empathy, and generosity. When we let God do the directing and we follow Jesus' perfect example, our days will be scripted with love, and joy will be the outcome!

FATHER, MAKE MY LIFE A PICTURE OF LOVE AND KINDNESS SO THE WORLD WILL SEE YOUR BEAUTY.

MAY 12

The Lord is fair in everything
He does and full of kindness.
PSALM 145:17

I wonder what our days would be like if we were to deny every urge to be impatient, grumbly, or ungrateful; if we would decide every morning to be *full of kindness* no matter what we encounter as the day unfolds. God is *always* kind to us Let's be kind, thankful, loving, and gentle...and give what we're given so freely.

FATHER, THANK YOU FOR YOUR
CONSTANT KINDNESS. SHOW ME WAYS
TO BE KIND TO OTHERS.

MAY 13

*Love each other in the same way
I have loved you.*
JOHN 15:12 NLT

Every day is a brand-new chance to bring
a little love into the world! The need is
everywhere, and God gladly guides us to
the opportunities He has for us. After all,
He created us and commands us to *love
each other*, to *interact*, to be *in relationships*. In that context, your tiniest acts of
kindness are sometimes the sweetest to
the recipient. Be kind when God nudges—
and be the difference in a person's life!

FATHER, LET ME BE THE REASON
SOMEONE SEES YOUR LOVE TODAY!

Show mercy and kindness to one another.
ZECHARIAH 7:9 NLT

There are endless ways to show people God's kindness and love—and eternal reasons to do so. *God is in our acts of kindness:* He is in every offer of forgiveness, every encouraging word, and every helping hand. In fact, He is the Originator of all that is good—and forgiveness, encouragement, and helping hands are all good. We are merely messengers wanting to share what we have received from Him. Now is the perfect time to shout it out and pour it on, with happy hearts and heavenly joy!

FATHER, GIVE ME A HEART THAT OVERFLOWS WITH YOUR GOODNESS AND REVEALS YOUR LOVE.

MAY 15

Spend your time in doing good.
Try to live in peace with everyone;
work hard at it.

PSALM 34:14

We all have hard days, those times when our do-good fire seems to have gone out, and there's nothing we can do to rekindle it. God understands. That's why He blesses us every morning with His fresh mercies and unfailing love. It's the double-dose of grace that we need when we feel weary from doing good. Let's receive that grace...and take in His fullness to refuel our souls.

FATHER, THANK YOU FOR BEING
MY STRENGTH AND COMFORT,
AND I'M GLAD YOU UNDERSTAND
THAT ON SOME DAYS I SIMPLY NEED
MORE OF YOU.

MAY 16

*Do you think anyone is going
to be able to drive a wedge between us
and Christ's love for us? There is no way!*
ROMANS 8:38 THE MESSAGE

The powerful, permeating, *present* love of
God is not going anywhere. It's beside us
during life's battles, beneath us when we
fall, ahead of us on our journey. No matter what direction we turn, we'll find ourselves in the thick of God's love—and very
thankful to be there. Love is why we're
here: God created us to be in relationship
with Him. Love is why Jesus came to this
planet: His death and resurrection defeated sin and restored our relationship with
God. And love is the message we have for
our dark and hurting world.

> FATHER, YOUR LOVE IS FAITHFUL,
> FERVENT, AND FOREVER. I PRAY
> IT SHINES BOLDLY AND BRIGHTLY
> THROUGH ME.

MAY 17

You are good and do only good;
make me follow Your lead.
PSALM 119:68

The more we learn to be still and listen for God's voice of love, the more often we will have opportunities to experience Him loving others through us. He's ready to lead us to the need—to the heart searching for hope; the friend afraid to say she's hurting; the coworker who could use a simple smile or kind word. God sees the unspoken, and then He speaks—through us—His kindness and love.

FATHER, HELP MY HEART LISTEN CLOSELY TO YOU SO THAT YOU CAN USE ME AS YOU WISH TO BLESS OTHERS WITH YOUR LOVE.

MAY 18

Remember the root command:
Love one another.
JOHN 15:17 THE MESSAGE

Love is the root of every beautiful word and action we extend and experience. All that we give for God's glory and all that we're given by His grace begins with love. So let's make love our priority today! Love is, after all, the *one thing* that changes *everything:* loving one another comforts our hearts, brightens our spirits, and brings health to our souls.

FATHER, I CHOOSE TO LOVE TODAY NO MATTER HOW I FEEL. I WILL RELY ON YOU TO HELP ME SHARE YOUR LOVE IN MY LITTLE SPOT IN THIS BIG WORLD.

MAY 19

There is treasure in being good.
PROVERBS 15:6

It's going to be a good day because our loving God is in it from beginning to end. God's love is here for us: it is hope for us, it is healing for us, and it is wholeness for us! The God we serve is *good, loving,* and *kind*. The greatest way to serve Him is to be like Him...*and that's a treasure worth seeking*.

FATHER, LET ME FIND JOY TODAY BY DOING GOOD, LOVING WELL, AND BEING KIND... JUST AS YOU DO.

MAY 20

We know how dearly God loves us,
because He has given us the Holy Spirit
to fill our hearts with His love.
ROMANS 5:5 NLT

God's Spirit fills our hearts with His love
so that we have love to share. As we both
ponder and share God's love, we appreciate more the depth of His sacrifice. We
can consider what the cross reveals of
God's character—of His grace, generosity, justice, righteousness, goodness, kindness, mercy, and, yes, love. When His loves
flows through, we grow too, and the more
we give, *the more blessed we live*.

FATHER, LET ALL I DO BE SATURATED
IN YOUR LOVE, AND LET MY LIFE BE AN
EVER-BRIGHTER REFLECTION OF YOU.

MAY 21

*Your beauty and love chase after me
every day of my life.*
PSALM 23:6 THE MESSAGE

God's love is on the move, seeking a home
in every heart. When God's love captures
and captivates us, we're called to carry
it into the world. The Lord can use the
way we treat others to soften hearts and
prompt people to *invite love in*. And once
His love overtakes us with beauty and
goodness, may we *never stop* sharing its
overflow with others.

FATHER, YOUR LOVE MAKES
ALL THINGS BEAUTIFUL AND
EVERY HEART WHOLE.
HELP ME LOVE WITH YOUR LOVE
THOSE WHO NEED A HEALED HEART.

MAY 22

Your love for Me will be in them,
and I will be in them.

JOHN 17:26 NLT

Our desire to truly love one another comes
when we have accepted Jesus as our Savior and, as a result, the Holy Spirit lives
within us. Jesus prayed for intimacy with
His followers, knowing it's the only way
God's love will prevail in our lives. We are
able to extend genuine love—to love when
it's difficult; be kind when we're frus-
trated; give when we feel empty; forgive
when we're hurting—only because God's
Spirit lives *within us*. When we lean into
His presence, love is *powerfully present*.

FATHER, THANK YOU FOR THE GIFT
OF YOUR SPIRIT WHO ENABLES ME TO
LOVE OTHERS WITH YOUR LOVE.

MAY 23

Cheerfully pleasing God is the main thing,
and that's what we aim to do.
II CORINTHIANS 5:9 THE MESSAGE

A life that is pleasing to God is all about love! Loving God most is the key to loving people more. There isn't a thing we need to add to our schedules or our to-do lists. Being kind when it's easier *not* to be; choosing to love despite a person's faults and failures; keeping our hearts free from dwelling on disappointments—developing love-winning habits like these may help win a soul and definitely brings a bigger smile to God!

FATHER, I'M HAPPIEST WHEN THE THINGS I DO PLEASE YOU. ME STRENGTH TO ALWAYS CHOOSE TO LOVE!

MAY 24

Wisdom from above is first of all pure.
It is also peace loving, gentle at all times,
and willing to yield to others.
JAMES 3:17 NLT

May we pray to *grow wise*. We are wise to acknowledge that the seeds of peace, a gentle spirit, and a willingness to put others first take time to bear fruit. Yielding to God's will—waiting for Him to transform our character—can sometimes feel like an unfair demand. But every time we *defer our needs* in order to serve with love, we *prefer the One* who loved us first—and *He* will always be our greatest reward!

FATHER, GIVE ME A HEART OF WISDOM
THAT UNDERSTANDS THE JOY OF
SERVING WITH LOVE.

MAY 25

Be gracious in your speech.
The goal is to bring out the best in others.
COLOSSIANS 4:6 THE MESSAGE

Light up a face with a word chosen well.
Lift up a heart with a story you tell.
Be the one wearing a comforting smile.
Be the one lending an ear for a while.
Say something kind to encourage
  a friend.
Do something kind; help a sorrow
  to mend.
Speak with compassion; keep love in
  your heart.
We'll brighten this world if we all do
  our part!

FATHER, MY BECOMING MORE LIKE
JESUS HAPPENS IN ME AS I DEPEND
ON YOU. FILL ME WITH YOUR SPIRIT
SO I AM MORE THE PERSON YOU
CREATED TO ME—AND SO I CAN SHINE
WITH YOUR LOVE.

MAY 26

He is the Lord our God.
His goodness is seen everywhere.
PSALM 105:7

God's goodness is seen everywhere, but may it be seen *abundantly* in you and me! Let our kindness draw others to Him and let our prayer be that they discover how *completely* they are loved! We're here to do the loving thing that could be the one thing that opens their heart to the One who is *everything*.

FATHER, ONE WAY YOUR GOODNESS FILLS THE EARTH IS BY SHINING THROUGH THE LOVE WE GIVE. THANK YOU FOR CHOOSING US TO LIGHT THE WAY FOR OTHERS.

MAY 27

*Keep on loving others
as long as life lasts.*
HEBREWS 6:11 NLT

On some days "keep on loving" sounds impossible. We are long on discouragement and short on patience. We have little energy to keep on going or to keep on loving. Our tank just seems empty. When we feel weak like this, may we remember that the One who is strongest will enable us to do what He has called us to do: He will enable us to "keep on loving others" despite our feeling of emptiness.

FATHER, EMPOWER ME TO LOVE THOSE
YOU CALL TO ME LOVE.

MAY 28

The eyes of the Lord are watching over
those who fear Him,
who rely upon His steady love.
PSALM 33:18

The steady, unchanging, unconditional love of God protects our souls from the harshness of this world—and His love the only protection. Our highest purpose is love God and other people. That means chores can wait if someone who is hurting needs us...if we can help carry a friend's burden...if a neighbor simply wants *someone there*. God is love, and trusting that He is with us, watching over us, enabling us to love, we're to reveal His amazing love.

FATHER, HELP ME REMEMBER THAT
NOTHING IN MY DAY IS MORE
IMPORTANT THAN SHARING YOUR LOVE.

MAY 29

Let no one seek his own [well-being],
but each one the other's well-being.
I CORINTHIANS 10:24 NKJV

Yes, we need to take care of ourselves, but God calls us to love and serve others to help ensure their well-being. We can be confident that our faithful God will not ignore our needs, freeing us to attend to the needs of others. What a privilege and joy to be able to love and serve others with God's love.

FATHER, THANK YOU THAT I CAN
SHARE YOUR LOVE AND SERVE OTHERS
JOYFULLY KNOWING THAT YOU WILL
FAITHFULLY MEET MY NEEDS.

MAY 30

*Make the most of every opportunity
you have for doing good.*
EPHESIANS 5:16

Today, let's look forward to the opportunities God gives us to *love someone with His love*. After all, that's why we're here! We are to stand with one another through the struggles, heartaches, and challenges of life. If we spend our time looking inward instead of looking outward with a heart sensitive to the needs of others, we miss too many chances for doing good—and too many divinely directed moments to show God's love!

FATHER, PREPARE MY HEART FOR
EVERY OPPORTUNITY TO DO GOOD BY
SHOWING PEOPLE YOUR LOVE.

MAY 31

There is nothing but goodness in Him!

PSALM 92:15

Oh, no one would ever describe us humans as "nothing but goodness"! That's one reason we need You, Lord. We need You to fill us with Your goodness through and through, so that the world can have the clearest view of You! We can—according to Your direction—do the simplest good deed and then watch You soften the hardest of hearts with Your love... just as You have softened ours.

FATHER, YOU ARE INCREDIBLY GOOD,
YOU ARE FOREVER FAITHFUL, AND
YOU ARE LOVE. LET MY LIFE FOCUS BE
REFLECTING YOU!

JUNE 1

Overwhelming victory is ours through Christ,
who loved us.
ROMANS 8:37 NLT

Impatience won't win today; anger won't have the last word; and discouragement won't keep us down. Jesus loves us, and His *love* is going to give us overwhelming, overcoming, overpowering victory over *everything* today! Jesus' love is going to shine through our smile, come alive through our actions, and give life through our words. God's light is going to brighten wherever we are in the world because of His love *within* us!

FATHER, YOU LOVE ME THE WAY I WANT
TO LOVE OTHERS. PLEASE ENABLE ME
TO DO SO.

JUNE 2

*God loves it when
the giver delights in the giving.*
II CORINTHIANS 9:7 THE MESSAGE

God loves to see us delight in giving because that's how He is with us! Our good and generous heavenly Father delights in giving us, His children, all we need and often far more. So may our days be filled with words and actions guided by the Holy Spirit and speaking strongly of God's *love*. Listening, being patient, staying positive, hugging long, paying attention—these are among the myriad ways we can show God's love throughout our days—and we can count on our endlessly loving Father to orchestrate the opportunities!

FATHER, SHOW ME WHO NEEDS YOUR LOVE TODAY, AND LET ME GIVE IT GLADLY AND GENEROUSLY.

JUNE 3

Always be joyful.
Never stop praying.
I THESSALONIANS 5:16-17 NLT

Joy and prayer just go together! Joy comes in our conversations with God, because there's *fullness of joy* in His very presence (Psalm 16:11). When in prayer we ask Him to set our spirits right for loving others, *He's right there to do it*. Our *always faithful* Father gives us the *always joyful* heart the world needs to see!

FATHER, FILL ME WITH JOY SO THE
WORLD WILL SEE THE LIGHT OF YOUR
LOVE AND PRESENCE IN ME.

JUNE 4

*Forgive one another as quickly
and thoroughly as God in Christ forgave you.*
EPHESIANS 4:32 THE MESSAGE

Quick and thorough forgiveness—that's a tough one for us. But it is the example that Jesus gives us, and it's a picture of how perfect love works. Jesus' death on the cross and His resurrection demonstrate God's great love for us and guarantee the thorough forgiveness of our sins. If we're going to love others by forgiving them "quickly and thoroughly," we're going to *have* to let go of offenses as if they were fire in our hands.

FATHER, THANK YOU FOR FORGIVING ME FULLY AND LOVING ME FAITHFULLY. LET MY FORGIVENESS AND LOVE OF OTHERS MIRROR YOURS.

JUNE 5

When the Holy Spirit controls our lives
He will produce this kind of fruit in us:
love, joy, peace, patience, kindness,
goodness, faithfulness,
gentleness and self-control.
GALATIANS 5:22-23

In the line-up of the fruit that results from the Holy Spirit's presence within us, love tops the list. Love is the preeminent fruit of a godly life. Love *changes hearts and, as a result, relationships, circumstances, and hopelessness.* Love shines the brightest spotlight on the beauty of God and draws hearts to *Him.*

FATHER, I CHOOSE TO LOVE TODAY,
AND I TRUST YOU, HOLY SPIRIT,
TO LEAD ME TO THOSE
WHO NEED IT MOST.

JUNE 6

Never tire of loyalty and kindness.
Hold these virtues tightly.
Write them deep within your heart.
PROVERBS 3:3

Maybe today, your heart is tired—from an ongoing struggle; from fighting to hold on to a thinning hope; or from feeling hurried through life day after day. But may your weariness not impact your commitment to loyalty and kindness. God is the Source of these traits as well as unlimited love, so turn to Him if you feel to tired to be kind. When we are weary, God enables us to continue to share His love by renewing our strength over and over again, and that's one of His *greatest* kindnesses to us.

FATHER, RENEW IN ME A KIND, STRONG, AND FAITHFUL SPIRIT SO THAT I CAN SERVE OTHERS WITH LOVE.

JUNE 7

Oh, how grateful and thankful
I am to the Lord because He is so good.
PSALM 7:17

A thankful heart is a loving heart. So let us be mindful every day of how *good* God is and be grateful for every person He brings into our lives to love. These people need us, and knowing they would, God brought them into our lives by design. His Spirit will guide us in *how* to love and enable us to love when it's hard. We can be grateful for that!

FATHER, I'M GRATEFUL FOR EVERY PERSON YOU PLACE IN MY LIFE, WHETHER FOR DECADES OR JUST MOMENTS. YOU ARE THE SOURCE OF THE LOVE THEY NEED. PLEASE LET YOUR LOVE FLOW THROUGH ME.

JUNE 8

*The Lord is good and
glad to teach the proper path
to all who go astray.*
PSALM 25:8

We're going to feel lovesick some days.
Those days occur when we've spent too
little time with our heavenly Father and
too much time dwelling on circumstances, fearing the future, or forgetting His
faithfulness. If you're feeling a bit lovesick
right now, know that God's arms are open
wide, and He is waiting for you to run inside. Maybe you can even sense Him whis-
pering to you, "I *love* you. I *value* you. I'm
here for you."

FATHER, STAYING CLOSE TO YOU
KEEPS MY HEART FREE FROM WORRY
AND FULL OF LOVE.

JUNE 9

He loves whatever is just and good;
the earth is filled with His tender love.
PSALM 33:5

One thoughtful, kind action can completely change someone's day. Be the one person who does the one kindness that makes *one soul* feel loved and valued! God's love has a tenderizing effect on the heart, and *softened* hearts make for a softer world. It's up to us to do the little things that God uses to make a big difference. In God's hands, one kind act at a time is plenty sufficient.

FATHER, USE MY HANDS AND MY HEART TO SHOW YOUR LOVE TO THE WORLD THROUGH KIND WORDS AND THOUGHTFUL ACTIONS.

JUNE 10

God is good to one and all;
everything He does is suffused with grace.
PSALM 145:9 THE MESSAGE

Love is simply and *thoroughly* good. It's not up to us to decide when to love or who deserves the goodness of God. If a person is in our life, for a moment or a longer part of the journey, it's our responsibility to treat them with love. As God choreographs lives to intersect, He is good to one and *all*—just as you and I should *always* be.

FATHER, GIVE ME THE DESIRE TO
CHOOSE TO LOVE AND BE GOOD TO
"ONE AND ALL."

JUNE 11

Great is His faithfulness;
His loving-kindness begins afresh each day.
LAMENTATIONS 3:23

Like waves to the shore
And the salty breeze,
Like birds sing in spring
From the tops of the trees,
Like mercies afresh
With every sunrise,
God's kindness is *ceaseless*.
You're *prized* in His eyes.

FATHER, NOTHING CAN STOP YOUR
LOVE FROM REACHING ME, YOUR
KINDNESS FROM COVERING ME, OR
YOUR FAITHFULNESS FROM CARRYING
ME. THANK YOU.

JUNE 12

Those who trust in the Lᴏʀᴅ
will lack no good thing.
PSALM 34:10 NLT

If we trust God, the psalmist sings, we won't lack *any* of the good things He gives—and we won't hesitate to *do good things* for others. The Holy Spirit will, for instance, *guide us*: He will , direct our steps, open our eyes, and soften our hearts to respond to a need. At other times the Spirit will bring to mind a specific person and give us a sense of urgency to pray. We are here to *be one of the good things of God* in the lives of other people.

FATHER, YOU ARE THE FAITHFUL
PROVIDER OF ALL WHO TRUST IN YOU.
KEEP ME AWARE TODAY OF WHO I
MIGHT INVITE TO PUT THEIR TRUST IN
YOU FOR THE FIRST TIME.

JUNE 13

The eyes of the Lord are intently watching all who live good lives, and He gives attention when they cry to Him.

PSALM 34:15

God's undivided attention is on those who reveal His undeniable goodness by the way they live their lives—and love is the *best* way to show how good God truly is! Love embodies many beautiful attributes of God. Love is kind, patient, selfless, forgiving, and full of compassion. When we act, react, and treat others according to this way of love, God sees...and is *seen*.

FATHER, MAKE ME A CHANNEL OF YOUR GOODNESS TODAY SO THAT SOMEONE MIGHT SEE A LITTLE MORE CLEARLY THE BEAUTY OF YOUR LOVE.

JUNE 14

I'll make a list of GOD's gracious dealings,
all the things GOD has done that need praising...
Compassion lavished, love extravagant.
ISAIAH 63:7 THE MESSAGE

Everything God does for us He does with love and grace. God's plans for us are *always* good; His compassion toward us will never fail. In the middle of the wait, the struggle, the suffering of our lives, God's love *covers* us, and His grace *carries* us. In time, we'll see that all His ways lead to blessings and praise!

FATHER, YOUR LOVE ALWAYS LEADS ME TO THE BEST, MOST BLESSED PLACE TO BE. KEEP ME FAITHFUL IN THANKING YOU AND PRAISING YOU IN THOSE PLACES.

JUNE 15

Drink deep of God's pure kindness.
Then you'll grow up mature and whole in God.
I PETER 2:3 THE MESSAGE

One sign of growth in our relationship with God is our kindness to others. The more we understand how loved we are by God Himself, the more of His love we'll be able to give! So let's try every day to grow a little deeper in our relationship with Him, so that in the days ahead we can love in bigger ways. God's kindness is pure... His love is perfect... and His purpose is for us to learn *from* and live *out* that purpose with kindness and love!

FATHER, YOUR KINDNESS AND YOUR LOVE ARE AMONG MY RICHEST BLESSINGS. FILL MY HEART WITH MORE OF YOU SO MY LOVE FOR OTHERS MAKES ME MORE LIKE YOU.

JUNE 16

*I am sure that God who began
the good work within you will keep right
on helping you grow in His grace.*

PHILIPPIANS 1:6

The love-grace connection is an imperative in our faith. We are to love even the unlovable, even our enemies, even those who have hurt us—and that kind of love is possible only with grace. The more we offer unmerited favor—grace—and extend love to the hard-to-love, the stronger our spiritual muscles become—and the greater God's influence in our lives and through our lives. If we stay mindful of the ultimate sacrifice He made for us—He gave His Son, Jesus, to die for you and for me—we'll more easily surrender *anything* that keeps us from treating others with our heavenly Father's kindness and love.

> FATHER, KEEP DOING YOUR GOOD
> AND LOVING WORK BOTH IN ME AND
> THROUGH ME. I SURRENDER ALL I AM
> SO THAT I CAN LOVE OTHERS WELL!

JUNE 17

I will praise the Lord
no matter what happens.
PSALM 34:1

Maybe you've never thought about it, but loving people is one of the purest ways we can praise God! No matter how we feel, no matter what we feel we deserve, and no matter what we believe others have done to *not* deserve our love and kindness, let's glorify God and love *anyway*. That's what He did for us. He gave it *all*, and *not at all* because we earned or deserved His infinite love, but because He loved us *anyway*.

FATHER, LET MY ACTIONS BE FILLED
WITH LOVE AND KINDNESS AND
THEREFORE BRING YOU PRAISE TODAY.

JUNE 18

Because of His kindness,
you have been saved through trusting Christ.
And even trusting is not of yourselves;
it too is a gift from God.
EPHESIANS 2:8

We can't take credit for the love we give or the kindness we show. Without the Spirit of God within, we are helpless to do what is *truly* good—the good that has an eternal impact. So let's trust God to make our love *matter* today. From the smallest gestures to the biggest sacrifices, each act of love will make a remarkable difference because of *the Holy Spirit within us*.

FATHER, I ASK YOU THAT YOUR SPIRIT WILL USE POWERFULLY THE LOVE AND KINDNESS I EXTEND TO OTHERS IN YOUR NAME.

JUNE 19

Live in harmony with each other.
ROMANS 12:16 NLT

Love should be given freely and without expectations. Our expectations can lead to disappointments, and those disappointments can lead to disharmony. It's tough to stay out of our emotions, but if we determine to stay close to God, we'll get closer to loving people the way He wants us to. And that is the way of extending mercy rather than remembering mistakes, offering compassion rather than counting up offenses, and—most important—remembering how much Christ loves *us*.

FATHER, I WANT TO LOVE OTHERS ACCORDING TO YOUR WILL, NOT MY EMOTIONS. GIVE ME THE WISDOM TO FOLLOW YOUR LEAD THAT I MAY LIVE IN HARMONY WITH OTHERS.

JUNE 20

Let Him have all your worries and cares,
for He is always thinking about you.
I PETER 5:7

Think about it. How can we do anything with the *fullness* of God's presence when we have worry taking up space in our hearts and minds? May we release those worries and embrace both the fullness of His presence and the joy it brings. Such joyfulness is a loving thing to bring into the world! We need more of it! Let's give God our cares, worries, and woes and walk with joy today no matter what does or doesn't go our way!

FATHER, I SURRENDER MY CARES TO YOU SO THAT I CAN BE MORE AWARE OF YOU. THANK YOU FOR NEVER TAKING YOUR MIND OFF OF ME!

JUNE 21

*Long before He laid down earth's foundations,
He had us in mind, had settled on us
as the focus of His love, to be made whole
and holy by His love.*

EPHESIANS 1: 4 THE MESSAGE

You are the *focus* of God's love! Everything good comes to you through that love-line, and every time you *do good* and *choose to love*, you turn the focus back on *Him*. That's what the world needs—*love that points people to Him, that leads people to Him!* After all, people need God's love every day in simple ways, difficult moments, and times of heartbreak and doubt. *You* know the love of God that brings comfort—and wholeness and holiness—to the hurting and the lonely. Don't hesitate to share the love that heals.

FATHER, THANK YOU FOR LOVING ME
BEFORE I WAS BORN...AND FOR MAKING
MY LIFE A CHANNEL OF YOUR LOVE.

JUNE 22

I am the light of the world.
So if you follow Me,
you won't be stumbling through the darkness,
for living light will flood your path.

JOHN 8:12

Your kindnesses shine with heaven's light because your spirit is ignited by Jesus, the Light of the world. The little things you do might not feel like they make a significant difference for God's work in this world, but by His grace, they *do*—so *always* do them! Let your heart follow His Spirit today. Say the kind word, send the encouraging note, be the good friend, and keep love's light shining!

FATHER, LET ME WALK IN HEAVEN'S
LIGHT BY FOLLOWING YOU—
AND LETTING YOUR LOVE SHINE
BRIGHTLY IN ALL I DO.

JUNE 23

*Your care for others is the measure
of your greatness.*
LUKE 9:48

Every single day we can wake up knowing that God wants us to love and care for the people in our lives. So let's make surrounding them with His love our top priority. Everything else can wait. Besides, many times it doesn't take a lot of time to meet a need. It just takes a little patience, a small pause for prayer, and a big love for God—because when we're loving others, we're loving *Him*.

FATHER, CARING FOR OTHERS
REFLECTS A GREATER LOVE FOR YOU,
AND ALL I WANT TO DO IS LEARN TO
LOVE YOU MORE.

JUNE 24

*If I have faith that says to a mountain, "Jump,"
and it jumps, but I don't love, I'm nothing.*
I CORINTHIANS 13:2 THE MESSAGE

It would be pretty *spectacular* to say,
"Jump" and watch a mountain do exactly that. But what would the point be?
It would draw attention to the one who
commanded the mountain, but would the
mere *spectacle* bring witnesses hope or
healing, comfort or purpose? Sometimes,
in our world of busyness and noise, an act
of love can be pretty *spectacular*—and it
absolutely can point recipients and witnesses to the Source of hope, healing,
comfort, and purpose.

FATHER, PLEASE HELP ME DO
EVERYTHING WITH LOVE.

JUNE 25

Oh, the joys of those
who are kind to the poor!
PSALM 41:1 NLT

Love can comfort the poor in spirit, kindness can soothe the wounded soul, and serving the poor can indeed bring joy. Love isn't always *hard* to share, but it does require a decision to be like Jesus in this *hardened* world. We're all walking through tough stuff; we're all carrying unspoken heartache and silently praying for the strength we need. So to love others we turn to God, the One who makes us *all* whole, and trust Him to love others through us.

FATHER, GIVE ME STRENGTH
TO SERVE—AND YOUR LOVE
TO LOVE OTHERS WITH—
WHENEVER I FEEL EMPTY.

JUNE 26

The L{ord takes care of the godly.
PSALM 37:17 NLT

God takes care of us. He provides everything we need to keep the light of His love shining in a dark world. On certain days—when our hearts feel empty and our energy spent—He will seem to be asking us to give more than we have. That's when we ask the Spirit to give us a heart of compassion to fuel what we want to do to keep God's love-light shining.

FATHER, THANK YOU FOR TAKING
CARE OF ME. THANK YOU FOR
STRENGTHENING ME TO DO ALL
YOU ASK OF ME TODAY—
AND TO DO IT WITH LOVE.

JUNE 27

Though the LORD is great,
He cares for the humble.
PSALM 138:6 NLT

There's no hierarchy in God's love. He freely gives His love to *all*. May our passionate prayer be to live and *give* with a heart as lavishly loving as His. We'll have many chances today to be generous with our time, kind with our speech, and patient when the pressure's turned up. As we care for others—society's humble, the neighbor, our family—the world sees *more* of God's love!

FATHER, I WANT TO LOVE OTHERS
WITHOUT ANY SENSE OF HIERARCHY,
WITHOUT PAUSE OR RESERVATION,
AND WITH A HEART OF HUMILITY
AND GRACE.

JUNE 28

Take tender care of those who are weak.
I THESSALONIANS 5:14 NLT

We are not superheroes of the faith every day. All of us are going to stumble, make mistake, doubt, worry, and even throw the occasional pity party. But on those tough days, God just may send some tender loving care your way. He's good about using His people to "take... care of those who are weak." He sees the hurting heart and sends the help. May we receive that blessing with gratitude—and be willing to be the strong one that's sent when another soul is spent.

FATHER, THANK YOU FOR YOUR GRACE THAT CARRIES ME THROUGH LIFE' WEARY DAYS. THANK YOU, TOO, FOR RENEWING MY STRENGTH— OFTEN THROUGH THE CARE OF A FELLOW BELIEVER— SO THERE ARE FEWER OF THOSE DAYS.

JUNE 29

*Work willingly at whatever you do,
as though you were working for the Lord
rather than for people.*
COLOSSIANS 3:23 NLT

Love like Jesus loves—*and love as if Jesus is the One standing in front of you*. Similarly, work like Jesus works, honoring His Father's commands—and work as if Jesus were your Boss. You see, God's love is fused with our purpose in this life. If we aren't sharing His love in all that we do, those efforts and accomplishments don't mean *anything*. Love is the *why* when we wake up every morning: why we're here and why we should be excited about *every chance* we have to give the heavenly love that's been given to us.

FATHER, HELP ME TO DO EVERYTHING WITH YOU IN MIND—AND WITH YOUR LOVE IN MY HEART!

JUNE 30

*How kind the L*ORD *is!*
How good He is!
So merciful, this God of ours!
PSALM 116:5 NLT

A life of love isn't a life of little resistance. Some days, love is the hardest thing to do. The enemy of our souls doesn't want us to succeed at looking like our heavenly Father by being kind, good, and merciful. But every single time we imitate Him, every wonderful thing about Him wins—and there isn't a single thing that can put out the light it brings!

FATHER, LET YOUR KINDNESS AND LOVE BRING LIGHT INTO THE WORLD THROUGH ME.

JULY 1

His compassion never ends.
LAMENTATIONS 3:22

There's no way to exhaust the compassion of God. When we do unlovable things we're not proud of or make mistakes we've made a hundred times before, we'll find God standing before us with His arms open wide. Run to the forgiveness and start again. It's the only way to give your heart the freedom to love others—and there's an incredible need for love right where you are today!

FATHER, YOUR ENDLESS COMPASSION
IS NEW EVERY MORNING,
RENEWING IN ME THE HEARTFELT
DESIRE TO LOVE OTHERS.

JULY 2

*It's in Christ that we find out who we are
and what we are living for.*
EPHESIANS 1:11 THE MESSAGE

No one knows you better than the One
who created you! He put a combination
of gifts in you that no one else on earth
has, and getting to know Him is the best
way for you to get to know you. Learning
to love God with all our hearts teaches us
to love others in all the right ways—with a
heart that's more and more like His.

FATHER, I WANT TO KNOW YOU MORE
AND LIVE A LIFE FILLED WITH PURPOSE
AND CENTERED IN CHRIST.

JULY 3

Kind words are like honey—
sweet to the soul and healthy for the body.
PROVERBS 16:24 NLT

Honey always prompts the thought of
sweetness, but in the Middle Eastern des-
ert, honey was almost as rare as it was
sweet. Of course kind words are sweet to
hear, sweet to a hurting heart, sweet to a
stressed-out mind and body. But in twen-
ty-first-century first-world nations, kind
words may be as rare as honey was in the
land of the writers of Proverbs more than
2000 years ago.

FATHER, SHOW ME WAYS TO BE KIND
TODAY. PLEASE GIVE ME THE WORDS
AND PROMPT ME TO ACT IN WAYS THAT
LIGHTEN SOMEONE'S BURDEN.

JULY 4

Try always to be led along together by the Holy Spirit and so be at peace with one another.
EPHESIANS 4:3

The greatest peace breaker may be our... tongues. We do damage to relationships and situations when we speak without first thinking and praying. When we pray, we are more likely to recognize and follow the Holy Spirit's leading. Following this simple rule can also encourage unity: pause and pray. Imagine what a difference in our relationships if we were to *pause and pray* before we speak. Before anger takes over. Before we communicate how offended we are. Before we call it quits. Before we complain. Let's teach ourselves to always pause and pray.

FATHER, HELP ME DEVELOP THE DISCIPLINE OF PAUSING AND PRAYING. THEN, I PRAY, GIVE ME THE COURAGE AND THE FAITH TO FOLLOW WHERE YOUR SPIRIT LEADS ME TODAY.

JULY 5

*I want you woven into a tapestry of love,
in touch with everything there is
to know of God.*

COLOSSIANS 2:2 THE MESSAGE

Imagine all of God's people "woven into a tapestry of love" and, with that, knowing all there is to know about Him. Knowing Him will mean knowing His love, for God is love. Staying close to God also keeps us mindful that love isn't based on feelings or what someone does or doesn't do. Wherever God has you and whomever you're with, kindness and love are *always* in order!

FATHER, THE WAY YOU LOVE ME IS THE GREATEST EXAMPLE OF HOW I SHOULD LOVE OTHERS. PREPARE MY HEART TO LOVE AND TO GIVE SELFLESSLY AND SACRIFICIALLY

JULY 6

Be humble,
thinking of others as
better than yourselves.
PHILIPPIANS 2:3 NLT

What a joy it is to experience the contentment that comes when we—as Christ did—
put the good of others first. Doing so is
not always our immediate reaction, nor is
it always easy— but "thinking of others"
is *always* what love does. If we get into
the habit of humility, we have less time
to worry about our own struggles. Focused on helping others, we see after we
have served that God has faithfully taken
care of us. He has loved us as we have
loved others.

FATHER, STRENGTHEN ME TO SERVE
WITH LOVE AND TO MAKE SACRIFICES
WITH JOY. PLEASE ALSO HELP ME
REMEMBER THAT AS I PUT OTHERS
FIRST, I LEARN TO TRUST YOU MORE.

JULY 7

I am the Lord your God,
who teaches you what is good for you
and leads you along the paths
you should follow.
ISAIAH 48:17 NLT

Most of us reading this book have probably done a lot of adulting, and we are clear about what is good for us and what paths we should follow. We may be clear, but we may clearly be wrong, We may also be getting in the way of what God wants for our lives. Yet giving up control is tough. Know, however, that God is faithful to guide us, He will provide what is good for us, and He paves the paths we should follow with His love.

> FATHER, GIVE ME THE DISCERNMENT
> I NEED TO GO IN THE DIRECTION OF
> WHAT'S BEST FOR MY LIFE—WHICH IS
> YOUR DIRECTION FOR MY LIFE. HELP
> ME TRUST YOUR LOVE ALONG THE WAY.

JULY 8

Give, and you will receive.
Your gift will return to you in full.
LUKE 6:38 NLT

Let's open the floodgates of love in our lives by *giving love away* with abandon every chance we get! We can be kind at home, courteous on the road, thoughtful when we're shopping, sensitive when we're talking to a friend—love is never off limits. And when we give our time and attention to people, making them feel valued, we find ourselves blessed and our lives enriched.

FATHER, OPEN MY EYES TO WAYS I CAN LOVE OTHERS AS I GO ABOUT MY DAY— AND GIVE ME A HEART THAT LOVES ABUNDANTLY.

JULY 9

His love has the first and last word
in everything we do.
II CORINTHIANS 5:14 THE MESSAGE

Love makes everything better. Actually, it makes everything the *best* it can possibly be. Smiles light up dark days, kindness lifts a discouraged heart, and a note left for a child, a teacher, or a coworker can contain life-giving words that are exactly what they need to hear. No act of love is ever a small thing. Some loving actions take just a tiny bit of effort, but the love communicated is *always* a big deal.

FATHER, TEACH ME TO ACT WHEN YOU PROMPT ME TO BLESS OTHERS WITH LOVE AND KINDNESS.

JULY 10

Love never gives up.
I CORINTHIANS 13:7 NLT

Do you thrive on change—or are you happy with your familiar rut? Wherever you fall on that spectrum, you know that change is inevitable. Circumstances change, and we change. Along the way, when we are stressed by the transition, we may be quite tough to love. But the one thing that carries us through *all* things is God's love. We couldn't make it through the ups and downs without it. God brings people to us at the right time, moves circumstances into place for His purposes, and leaves traces of His faithful, forever love every step of the way. God's love for us truly is a love that "never gives up."

FATHER, I THANK YOU THAT YOUR LOVE NEVER GIVES UP ON ME. PLEASE HELP ME KNOW WHEN IT'S APPROPRIATE FOR ME TO EXTEND NEVER-GIVES-UP LOVE—AND THEN ENABLE ME TO DO SO.

JULY 11

Let love guide your life.
COLOSSIANS 3:14

God's love is the best guide when it comes to navigating this fallen world. Although our journeys and our battles are different, each one of us will handle both better when we "let love guide." Let God's love also guide what you do and say. He uses such sharing of His love to draw people into a saving knowledge of Him.

FATHER, PLEASE TEACH ME
TO LET YOUR LOVE GUIDE ME IN
EVERYTHING I DO.

JULY 12

We can make our plans,
but the final outcome is in God's hands.
PROVERBS 16:1

Although it may seem so at times, our lives aren't a collection of random events. Our sovereign God is in control, and because God is love, we can be confident that He exercises His control over our hours and our years with wisdom and love. Choices we make and plans we try to execute along the way might slow down our progress, but God's love for you will not lapse for any part of your journey. God's love isn't fickle... His love is *faithful*. So we can make our plans, but we can also trust the God who holds the final outcome in His hands.

FATHER, THANK YOU FOR YOUR LOVE THAT BROUGHT ME TO LIFE, REFUSES TO GIVE UP ON ME, AND LEADS ME TO YOUR BEST!

JULY 13

With His love,
He will calm all your fears.
ZEPHANIAH 3:17 NLT

The things we go through go better when we're calm. And God uses His *love* to calm our fears, our frustrations, and any form of frenzy that try to makes its way into our day! God's love will *always* win if we let it in. His love will soothe our nerves and slow our anger, clear our minds and carry our worries. God's love has got us—and everything is going to be OK.

FATHER, YOUR LOVE IS WITH ME, SO
I WILL GET THROUGH THE DAY IN A
PEACEFUL WAY.

JULY 14

Create in me a clean heart, O God.
Renew a loyal spirit within me.
PSALM 51:10 NLT

Our hearts can harbor the wrong things—unspoken apologies, unforgiveness, unreleased fears. Things very *unlike* God. But His hands that created us can also create a clean heart *within* us. He can lift every weight holding us down and wipe away the negativity clouding our purpose—which is *first* and *always* to *love one another*. So let's start our day by asking God for a spotless heart ready to shine with His love!

FATHER, I GIVE YOU EVERYTHING IN ME THAT DOESN'T GLORIFY YOU, SO THAT I CAN LOVE OTHERS BETTER.

JULY 15

God is sheer mercy and grace;
not easily angered, He's rich in love.
PSALM 103:8 THE MESSAGE

Even on rough days when we aren't pay-ing attention to God's presence or notic-ing the love He shows us in little ways and big, our responses—or lack thereof—don't dictate His faithfulness. He's right there in the thick of things with love that moves mountains, mends our brokenness, minis-ters to our wounds, and makes us whole. Take a moment when life takes the wind out of you and breathe in His awesome love for you. *It's there to get you through.*

FATHER, YOUR LOVE IS WHAT I NEED IF I'M GOING TO LOVE OTHERS WELL.

JULY 16

*Admit your faults to one another
and pray for each other
so that you may be healed.*

JAMES 5:16

An apology is an act of love. Offered with humility, it helps the healing of those we've hurt. When apologies don't come when we've been hurt, our love can be caged. Then, if we don't keep our hearts clear of bitterness, we that to withdraw and become preoccupied with *our* need and *our* pain. So let's give apologies sincerely and receive them gracefully, so love can always flow freely.

FATHER, LET ME BE HUMBLE AND QUICK TO APOLOGIZE—NEVER AFRAID TO FACE MY FAULTS—SO I CAN RECEIVE THE HEALING POWER OF YOUR LOVE.

JULY 17

*Our lives are a Christ-like fragrance
rising up to God.*
II CORINTHIANS 2:15 NLT

Christ-like looks like *love.* If our lives are going to show the world what His life brings us, we need to bring the love! And Christ-like love is kind. It's not easily offended. It's bright, encouraging, and winsome. It draws hearts to Him and openly welcomes *anyone* regardless of their present or their past. Let's be something God is pleased to see—a fragrance that attracts people to His Son!

FATHER, HELP ME TREAT OTHERS
KINDLY WANT WITH A WINSOME LOVE
THAT DRAWS THEM TO YOU!

JULY 18

*Don't do your good deeds publicly,
to be admired, for then you will lose
the reward from your Father in heaven.*

MATTHEW 6:1

Being kind shouldn't be something we wake up in the morning and decide to do. Instead, being kind and loving should be *who we are*...because of *whom we belong to*. So may we love and extend kindness for our Father in heaven, not for the praise of people. May all we do be influenced by God's love for His glory and for the good of those He loves through us.

FATHER, HELP ME TO LOVE FOR YOUR GLORY, NOT FOR PUBLIC ACKNOWLEDGMENT OR PRAISE.

JULY 19

No matter what I say,
what I believe, and what I do,
I'm bankrupt without love.
I CORINTHIANS 13:2 THE MESSAGE

If I stack up all the gold and silver
Found in all the earth;
If my skills command a fancy wage,
Three hundred billion dollars worth;
If I have the means to buy the things
Of all my hopes and dreams,
But don't invest my life in love—
It won't be worth a hill of beans.

FATHER, LOVE IS EVERYTHING.
ENABLE ME TO SHARE YOUR LOVE IN
ALL THAT I DO.

JULY 20

*Fix your attention on God.
You'll be changed from the inside out.*
ROMANS 12:2 THE MESSAGE

Inside changes make our outside brighter—especially when God is doing that inside job! Furthermore, our actions follow whatever we give attention to day after day, so when we choose to look to God and see how *faithful* He is, we more readily yield our hearts to Him and receive from Him His goodness and grace. Focusing on Him fine-tunes our spirit—and changes us from the inside out!

FATHER, SEARCH MY HEART AND CHANGE WHAT NEEDS TO CHANGE. PLEASE SHOW ME WHAT I NEED TO DO TO COOPERATE WITH YOU IN THAT WORK. I WANT MY LIFE TO SHINE FOR YOU.

JULY 21

If your gift is to encourage others,
be encouraging. If it is giving,
give generously.
ROMANS 12:8 NLT

The gifts God has given you are ways for you to share His love! You're not like anyone else, and God will use your unique set of traits to bless others. *And blessing others is loving others.* Your heart will lead you to do things another person might not think of, and vice versa. Running through all our gifts is the common thread of love—and we need it, and we're happier when we give it, because God is always in it.

FATHER, THANK YOU FOR THE SPECIAL GIFTS YOU'VE GIVEN ME. MAY I ALWAYS USE THEM TO LOVE OTHERS.

JULY 22

*Oh, the joys of those
who are kind to the poor!*
PSALM 41:1 NLT

Kindness is one of the clearest reflections of God's love. We have the privilege—several times a day—of bringing His kindness into the world, and *that* guarantees joy! We don't need to perform mountain-moving feats. The smallest act of kindness, done with thoughtfulness and love, can have a huge impact on those who are economically, emotionally, or relationally poor. We don't get to *see* the lasting impression our kindness makes on a heart, but God does—and it fills *Him* with joy too!

FATHER, FILL ME WITH YOUR KINDNESS
AND LOVE AND MAY I KNOW
YOUR JOY AS I LET IT OVERFLOW
INTO THE WORLD!

JULY 23

*Love cares more for others
than for self.*
I CORINTHIANS 13:5 THE MESSAGE

So often we feel exhausted as we juggle the daily pressures of appointments, to-do lists, and the unending tasks of running a household. Where do we find the time, energy, emotional stamina, and spiritual strength to care for others? *We look to God and depend on Him*—on His strength in our weakness, His power in our emptiness, and His amazing love in our choice to fulfill His *highest* purpose... which is *showing His heart to others*.

FATHER, FILL ME WITH THE FULLNESS OF YOUR SPIRIT SO I CAN LOVE AND SERVE OTHERS IN NEED.

JULY 24

As for others,
help them find the Lord
by being kind to them.
JUDE 1:23

Our words don't always make an impression on people who don't know the love of God, but what we do, *does*. An act of kindness is seen, felt, and *remembered* when it is infused with love. Love leads hearts to God, and hearts that find true love in Him are truly changed. There's nothing more sure or secure than the love of Jesus—and the more we show it, the brighter the world!

FATHER, MAKE ME A BRIGHT LIGHT FOR THOSE WHO NEED YOUR TRUE AND PERFECT LOVE.

JULY 25

You can be sure that God
will take care of everything you need.
PHILIPPIANS 4:19 THE MESSAGE

Our love-needs are met in full—actually, to overflowing measure—by the God we serve. So let's not hesitate to pour it out on everyone in our lives! God has you where He needs you, with people who need to see and be touched by His love. Children are learning about God's love...friends are depending on it...strangers are searching for it. We have an *incredible* responsibility—and He has the grace to provide His love and guide us as we share it.

FATHER, GIVE ME YOUR LOVE,
THE LOVE I NEED IN ORDER TO LOVE
EVERYONE IN MY LIFE FULLY
AND FAITHFULLY.

JULY 26

There are three things that remain—
faith, hope, and love—
and the greatest of these is love.

I CORINTHIANS 13:13

Love is great, and God is good—and those are the *only* things we need to remember and reflect if we want to serve God and honor Him with our lives. Nothing else matters much, because God's love goes straight to the heart of a matter and makes the lasting difference. God will give us the perfect word for the broken spirit, the generosity that meets the need, the helping hand that saves the day. Love *never* fails.

FATHER, LOVE IS THE GREATEST
REFLECTION OF YOU IN THIS DARK
WORLD OF NEED. LET ME SHINE
THE LIGHT OF YOUR LOVE.

JULY 27

Love is very patient and kind...
Love does not demand its own way.
I CORINTHIANS 13:4-5

Smile. *That's love.* Say *thank you. That's love.* Call a friend, help a neighbor, write a note—go out of your way to put love in someone's day. We're *here* on this earth to *love.* Most important, we are to love the One who created us...and then we are to love the ones He *brings* to us.

FATHER, GIVE ME A HEART GRATEFUL
FOR YOUR LOVE, A HEART THAT
DAILY GROWS MORE GENEROUS
WITH THAT LOVE.

JULY 28

*He made the world
and everything in it.*
ACTS 17:24

From our families and friends to those
people we meet by surprise or circumstance, God has a reason our paths cross,
and His reason is *always* love. Love is our
highest calling and our greatest purpose,
so God directs our steps to the people and
places of His choosing where He trusts us
to reveal His heart. When our actions are
powered by love, our lives point others
to Him.

FATHER, I WANT YOU TO BE WHAT
OTHERS SEE IN ME AS YOU ENABLE ME
TO LIVE WITH LOVE, HUMILITY,
AND KINDNESS.

JULY 29

Let Your tenderhearted mercies
meet our needs.
PSALM 79:8

God understands when we're emotionally
out of gas. It happens when we choose to
be kind in an often unkind world, sometimes without appreciation or reciprocation. It happens as we help meet other
people's needs, again without appreciation or reciprocation. *When we get weary*
and our spirits wear out, His love rushes
in...and His tenderhearted mercies fill
us again.

FATHER, I OPEN MY HEART TO YOUR
TENDER MERCIES, GRATEFUL THAT YOU
FAITHFULLY REFUEL MY SPIRIT WITH
YOUR MIGHTY LOVE.

JULY 30

As high as heaven is over the earth,
so strong is His love to those who fear Him.
PSALM 103:11 THE MESSAGE

We can't love the world into the arms of God until He means more than the world to us! When God holds first place in our lives, His love is strong in us and through us. We find it easier to get out of the way and let Him have His way, and when that happens, love has taken over. We shine a little brighter, spread joy a little wider, and see what matters a whole lot clearer.

FATHER, YOU ARE LOVE—AND MAY YOU, MAY LOVE, COME FIRST IN MY LIFE. I PRAISE YOU FOR YOUR LOVE AND FOR THE UNENDING GRACE AND GOODNESS YOU ALSO POUR INTO MY LIFE.

JULY 31

*Life is worth nothing unless I use it for doing
the work assigned me by the Lord Jesus—
the work of telling others the Good News
about God's mighty kindness and love.*
ACTS 20:24

The power of God's kindness and love is
indisputable. When God uses us to pour
it into the lives of others, we can watch it
give courage, hope, and strength. We see
His mighty kindness and love prompt gratitude and bring joy. In fact, love doesn't
have any negative side effects. Everything
it sets in motion is *good*, and our purpose
is to tell the world how good God is with
our words and by the way we treat others.
Whatever the means, may we *always* deliver the message with love.

FATHER, BLESS MY HANDS AND MY
HEART FOR THE WORK OF YOUR
SPIRIT, SO OTHERS WILL KNOW THE
POWER OF YOUR LOVE.

AUGUST 1

*My love won't walk away
from you.*
ISAIAH 54:10 THE MESSAGE

An ocean of God's love stretches out in front of you. A sky full of His love reaches above you. A mountain of love towers beside you, and His shield of love surrounds you. God's love is everlasting, all encompassing, and always with you. His love doesn't walk away. God's love *stays* even when your hope runs low, your stress runs high, and your strength runs out.

FATHER, THANK YOU FOR SAVING AND STRENGTHENING ME WITH YOUR INFINITE LOVE—AND THANK YOU THAT YOUR LOVE STAYS.

AUGUST 2

Don't look out only for your own interests,
but take an interest in others, too.
PHILIPPIANS 2:4 NLT

Is this what your days look like—at least sometimes? You wake up tired, are busy all day, and then go to bed with more to do than you had when the sun came up. And still you want to give more, to serve God more, to be more like Jesus. But right now just sit quietly and bask in God's love for you. Let these moments with Him remind you how close He is and how much bigger His grace is than *anything* you go through. (Jesus Himself got away with God just like this!)

FATHER, YOU HEAR THE CALL OF MY HEART, AND YOU ARE FAITHFUL TO ANSWER. MAKE ME STRONG WHEN I'M WEAK AND RESTORE MY SPIRIT WITH YOUR JOY!

AUGUST 3

*Forget yourselves long enough
to lend a helping hand.*
PHILIPPIANS 2:4 THE MESSAGE

It's hard to imagine our minds *not* being on overload. We're constantly bombarded by screens, scrolling, and sound bites. And then there's the noise of the stuff we actually need to do. And then, also calling our name, are those things we know we *should* do. Pray for someone we know is going through a tough time; make a meal for a friend; help the new mommy; write the overdue thank-you note; and, basically, *be a blessing by showing God's love.*

FATHER, TURN MY FOCUS TO THE NEEDS AROUND ME—AND THEN SHOW ME WHERE AND HOW YOU WANT ME TO SHARE YOUR LOVE.

AUGUST 4

God is the faithful God
who for a thousand generations keeps
His promises and constantly loves those
who love Him.

DEUTERONOMY 7:9

God's love is constant, consistent, and compassionate. The power of His perfect love should be our pursuit. If we get to the place where we understand even a fraction of how *good* His love is, our heart's deepest desire will be sharing it with others. We won't see how far our kindness goes, but the love that fuels kindness plants a seed of possibility. God just may use the kindness of His people to guide someone to eternal life with Him.

FATHER, YOUR LOVE HOLDS
THE POWER TO TRANSFORM HEARTS
AND CHANGE THE WORLD.
MAY IT FLOW THROUGH ME!

AUGUST 5

*We all have the same God and Father
who is over us all and in us all,
and living through every part of us.*
EPHESIANS 4:6

We human beings sure can complicate things. For instance, God says, "Don't worry about how the day unfolds. Walk with Me and *just be*." But do we really grasp what that means and accept it? We don't have to go searching for what we should be doing with our lives. If we believe God is in control—and He is, we can rest assured that we are *exactly* where we need to be and that those people who need our gifts, our time, and *His love* are right in front of us.

FATHER, I'LL SURRENDER TO YOU AND NOT STRIVE TODAY, ASKING YOU AND TRUSTING YOU TO TEACH ME HOW TO SIMPLY WALK WITH YOU AND JUST BE.

AUGUST 6

Oh, what a wonderful God we have!
ROMANS 11:33

Think about how you would follow up that joy-filled statement of praise.... After this exclamation, the apostle Paul celebrated not only the greatness of God's "wisdom and knowledge and riches" but also "how impossible it is for us to understand his decisions and methods" (v. 33). And that impossibility is a good thing because it implies that, however big our Goliaths, God is always bigger. That message may be words of love and hope for someone you see today.

FATHER, YOU TRULY ARE A WONDERFUL GOD—AND A BIG GOD, BIGGER THAN THE HURTS I'VE ENDURED AND THE CHALLENGES I FACE. THANK YOU FOR LOVING LITTLE ME.

AUGUST 7

The Lord directs the steps of the godly.
He delights in every detail of their lives.
PSALM 37:23 NLT

When God's people—when you and I—consult Him at a crossroads of their lives or ask Him to help us make an important decision, He will gladly direct our steps. After all, our Creator and heavenly Father loves us and "delights in every detail of [our] lives." So may we keep our hearts sensitive to the Holy Spirit's direction. On a big scale, He will direct us at major decision points, and at the same time on a smaller scale, He will direct us to people who need a touch of God's kindness and love.

FATHER, LET MY LIFE BE A LIGHT THAT SHINES FORTH THE BEAUTY OF YOUR LOVE AND GOODNESS FOR PEOPLE TO SEE AND TO DESIRE.

AUGUST 8

Your love, GOD, took hold and held me fast.
When I was upset and beside myself,
You calmed me down and cheered me up.
PSALM 94:18-19 THE MESSAGE

Sit for a bit with God and *recharge*. Let His love for you do what it does best: remind you of such key truths as you are valuable, your life has purpose, you don't have to do a thing to earn God's acceptance or His forgiveness—and you have some things to do today. To be specific, you are use the unique gifts He's given you for the good of others and for His glory. So put your plans in His hands and enjoy the blessings He'll bring!

FATHER, GUIDE MY DAY WITH YOUR TRUTH AND LOVE, AND LET ME BE A BLESSING TO OTHERS.

AUGUST 9

*This is what God does. He gives His best—
the sun to warm and rain to nourish—
to everyone, regardless.*

MATTHEW 5:45 THE MESSAGE

When it comes to being kind, let's follow the Regardless Rule: whether or not we think it's deserved, no matter how badly we've been treated; whatever our mood or however our day is going—regardless, we can trust that God is giving us His best. Since God blesses everyone with, for instance, sun and rain *regardless*, the only way for us to accurately reflect His love in this world is to do the same is to extend grace to people, *regardless of what they've done.*

FATHER, YOU DO NOT WITHHOLD YOUR GOODNESS FROM ANYONE. HELP ME BE KIND AND LOVING WITH THE SAME POINTING-TO-JESUS WILLINGNESS AND GRACE.

AUGUST 10

Ever since the world was created,
people have seen the earth and sky.
Through everything God made,
they can clearly see His invisible qualities.

ROMANS 1:20 NLT

God's act of Creation was thoroughly and completely an act of love. Consider His love notes to you every day. Maybe one of today's was a beautiful blue sky, a flower in bloom, or a gorgeous sunset. The God-created things that make you feel thankful can at the same time speak to your heart and remind you of His infinite goodness and His amazing grace. We also experience a touch of God's goodness and grace when we choose to treat others with love.

FATHER, JUST AS ALL THAT YOU MADE REVEALS YOUR INVISIBLE QUALITIES— YOUR POWER, YOUR MAGNIFICENCE, YOUR GLORY, YOU SOVEREIGNTY, AND SO MUCH MORE—MAY ALL THAT I DO REVEAL YOUR LOVE.

AUGUST 11

*You must love the L<small>ORD</small> your God
with all your heart, all your soul,
and all your mind.*

MATTHEW 22:37 NLT

Loving the Lord with all our minds? That isn't an easy assignment! One reason is that the landscape of our minds can be a cluttered, noisy, and unsettled place—but it doesn't have to stay that way. Giving God control—yielding our thoughts to Him—can clear it out. *Give Him full rein today.* Let Him have the thing you don't think you can let go of. Surrender your hurts and pick up His hope. *Peace will come, joy will surface, strength will emerge, and your soul will rest.* These are some of the fruits of loving Him most and leaning in close.

> FATHER, PLEASE TAKE AWAY ANYTHING
> IN ME THAT EITHER GETS IN THE WAY
> OF MY LOVING YOU OR KEEPS ME
> FROM RECEIVING THE FULLNESS OF
> WHO YOU ARE.

AUGUST 12

God is working in you,
giving you the desire and
the power to do what pleases Him.
PHILIPPIANS 2:13 NLT

God calls us to share the light of His love in this dark and hurting world—but *we're not in this alone*. We don't impart kindness, or love without condition, or live for the glory of God without His help. And that's how He planned it. He didn't assign us a divine purpose and then leave us to figure it out as we go. Instead, by the power of His Spirit, God is at work within us *every day*. That's no ordinary thing, even on ordinary days. What we experience as a routine is actually a *refining* for greater things ahead!

FATHER, THANK YOU FOR GIVING ME THE DESIRE AND POWER TO PLEASE YOU WITH MY OBEDIENCE, MY WORSHIP, AND MY LOVE.

AUGUST 13

He is the living God,
and steadfast forever.
DANIEL 6:26 NKJV

It's hard to resist following our feelings. They can be impacted by so many things, and they pull us in different directions every day. But our steadfast God gives us the stability we need when He makes promises of faithfulness, guarantees our forgiveness, and welcomes us into His forever family. The living God is our hope for a stable life, one that isn't swayed by circumstances, emotions, or the actions of others. Jesus is the Rock on which we build our lives.

FATHER, THANK YOU FOR YOUR STEADFAST LOVE AND FAITHFULNESS. MAY I BUILD MY LIFE ON MY RELATIONSHIP WITH YOU, RECEIVING YOUR LOVE, GUIDED BY YOUR LOVE, AND SHARING YOUR LOVE.

AUGUST 14

God is not unjust to forget your work
and labor of love which you have shown
toward His name.
HEBREWS 6:10 NKJV

We can feel exhausted from serving all
week at vacation Bible school. Our hearts
can feel a bit pummeled after an after-
noon of tutoring at the city's afterschool
program. In many such circumstances, we
just may wonder if what we do out of love
and kindness is making a difference. In
times like that, *know this*: God sees all and
forgets nothing. Not an ounce of the love
you give falls to the ground without bear-
ing fruit. And these acts of love don't just
make an *undeniable* difference here, but
they make an *indelible* mark in eternity.

FATHER, GIVE ME STRENGTH TODAY
TO DO YOUR WILL, TO FULFILL MY
HIGHEST PURPOSE IN LIFE... WHICH IS
SHOWING OTHERS YOUR LOVE.

AUGUST 15

Your attitude must be like My own,
for I... did not come to be served,
but to serve.
MATTHEW 20:28

God sent Jesus, the ultimate Servant who died for our sins. God sends us to serve as Jesus did—and remember that He washed His disciples' feet? Serving others is the only way to a fulfilled life because we will be doing what God asks us to do. Doing what pleases Him blesses us! We're called to love and serve, to care and be kind, and to rely on God for the strength we need. Living to serve might not always be the easiest path in life, but it will always lead to the greatest—and an eternal—reward.

FATHER, SERVING YOU FAITHFULLY MEANS SERVING OTHERS WILLINGLY. SO PLEASE SOFTEN MY HEART AND STRENGTHEN MY BODY SO THAT I AM ABLE TO DO ALL YOU ASK OF ME.

AUGUST 16

GOD's love... is ever and always,
eternally present to all who fear Him.
PSALM 103:17 THE MESSAGE

Even when we don't feel God's love or
see it in the people around us or notice
it in the miracles of nature, His love truly
is ever and always *present.* God wraps His
love around us with His everlasting arms,
and beneath us He provides the rock of
His might. God's love is not going anywhere, and it's needed everywhere—so
let's bring it to life and into the spotlight
every chance we get.

FATHER, I PRAISE YOU FOR YOUR EVER-
PRESENT AND VERY POWERFUL LOVE.
LET MY LIFE BE AN EVER CLEARER
REFLECTION OF IT.

AUGUST 17

Live in peace with each other.

MARK 9:50

We all lose our tempers. Someone uses up our last ounce of patience—and off we go! But as quickly as we fall, we can pray. And just as quickly God forgives us and restores us. That steady, calming river of love never stops flowing from His heart into our lives, and its underlying current is *grace*. The more we let His mercy wash over us, the more His peace will rule in our lives.

FATHER, GIVE ME GRACE FOR THE TOUGH DAYS AND STRENGTH TO WALK IN LOVE WHEN THOSE DAYS COME.

AUGUST 18

Love each other just as much as I love you.
JOHN 13:34

That's a beautiful goal to try and reach in life, to love like Jesus. We'll spend our days never reaching the height or depth of it, we'll only be able to love others His way by depending on His power. It's a good thing we have it! And learning to lean on Him more will lead to us loving Him more, which will result in us loving others better.

FATHER, FILL ME WITH
THE POWER OF YOUR LOVE TODAY,
SO I CAN LOVE OTHERS IN THE BEST,
MOST CHRIST-LIKE WAY.

AUGUST 19

*Throw yourselves into the work of the Master,
confident that nothing you do for Him is
a waste of time or effort.*

I CORINTHIANS 15:58 THE MESSAGE

We all want to make a difference in this
world—and if the difference is going to
last beyond our lifetime, *love is required.*
We need to throw ourselves into the work
of kindness, the habit of forgiveness, the
deeds of goodness, and the actions of
love. None of these will fade or fail because they are guided and blessed by God
Himself, who is love.

FATHER, FILL MY HEART WITH YOUR
LOVE SO THAT ALL I DO IS INFUSED
WITH YOUR GOODNESS AND LOVE.

AUGUST 20

*Each of us will be a blessing
to the other.*
ROMANS 1:12

We were created by God to *be a blessing*.
And one way we can do that is to love people. In fact, we *never* lack opportunities to
love others. There will always be someone
to serve, encourage, listen to, hug, smile
at, cry with, or care for. Someone to bless.
If we aren't *there* for each other, then
we've forgotten why we're *here*—and we'll
never know the truest joy of living.

FATHER, LET ME BE A BLESSING
WHEREVER YOU LEAD TODAY. I
WOULD ASK YOU TO SHOW ME WHO
IS IN NEED OF A TOUCH OF YOUR
UNCONDITIONAL LOVE, BUT THAT IS
PRETTY MUCH EVERYONE.

AUGUST 21

*Encourage each other
to build each other up.*
I THESSALONIANS 5:11

Ours is a broken, battered world, and it can keep us heartbroken if we let it. So let's not let it. Instead, let's *be good* to each other and show one another what God's love looks like. It looks like a smile and a helping hand, a hug and taking time to pray. Love looks like serving, listening, being there, and *believing God is there too*. Love gets stronger when we give it—and brighter when we live it.

FATHER, GIVE ME THE WORDS TO SPEAK AND THE WISDOM TO ADDRESS THE NEED, SO THAT YOUR LOVE SHINES BRIGHTLY THROUGH ME.

AUGUST 22

When you help someone out,
don't think about how it looks. Just do it—
quietly and unobtrusively.
MATTHEW 6:4 THE MESSAGE

There are times when the Spirit of God will speak to our hearts, nudging us to meet a need or help someone out, and we'll hesitate to follow through. But part of growing in our relationship with our heavenly Father is learning to serve without hesitation or fear. When we give, *God's love is there*—and His love not only blesses the one receiving it but it also builds the faith of the one giving it.

FATHER, TEACH ME TO BE SENSITIVE
TO YOUR SPIRIT AND WILLING
TO SHARE YOUR LOVE WITHOUT
HOLDING BACK.

AUGUST 23

Aim for harmony...
and try to build each other up.
ROMANS 14:19

Encouragement is a sweet language of love, and it's so easy to give! When we think of a kind thing to say, we need to simply give it voice. We can make a phone call, send a text, or write a note. A small act of thoughtfulness can be a big deal in someone's day—and chances are that this love in action will create a ripple effect of *joy*.

FATHER, GIVE ME WISDOM TO SHARE
WORDS OF ENCOURAGEMENT TODAY,
TO LET ONE OR TWO PEOPLE KNOW
THAT YOU HOLD THEM IN YOUR
PERFECT LOVE.

AUGUST 24

Examine me, GOD...
Make sure I'm fit inside and out
so I never lose sight of Your love.
PSALM 26:2-3 THE MESSAGE

Exercise keeps the body fit to *live*... the same way prayer keeps the spirit fit to *love*. Asking God to show us how our hearts need to change—and then cooperating with Him as He helps us make those changes—will keep our actions reflecting His love. We definitely need that inside fitness if the world is going to see—and seek—what we have in Him!

FATHER, PLEASE HELP ME BECOME
MORE A PERSON OF PRAYER:
I WANT TO WALK THROUGH THE DAY
IN CONVERSATION WITH YOU. I WANT
THE LIGHT OF YOUR LOVE SHINING
BRIGHTLY IN MY LIFE.

AUGUST 25

God will generously provide all you need.
Then you will always have everything you need
and plenty left over to share with others.

II CORINTHIANS 9:8 NLT

It's a basic truth: *Love comes from God.* And when He calls us to put our love into action, He will never ask us to give something He hasn't already given to us. For instance, He created each of us with *unique gifts*. Some of us might be patient listeners. Others might be diligent servers. Still others are great at encouraging and restoring hope to a heart. You know *you*, and you know the gifts God has given you. Know, too, that the world needs *your* expression of love!

FATHER, THANK YOU FOR THE GIFTS
YOU'VE GIVEN ME FROM THE WEALTH
OF YOUR LOVE. HELP ME USE THEM
TO SHARE YOUR LOVE AND
BRING YOU GLORY.

AUGUST 26

Strength comes straight from God.
PSALM 62:11 THE MESSAGE

There's a perfect strength, streaming straight from heaven to our spirits. Not only were we created *not* to do life alone, but *we never have to*. When we feel weak and worn out from daily pressures, may this emptiness prompt us to take some time to be with Him. He knows exactly what we need, and we need to let Him re-energize us for the work of His heart in the world—*loving people with His love*.

FATHER, RESTORE MY STRENGTH THAT I MIGHT—IN LOVE—GIVE WHAT YOU HAVE CREATED ME TO GIVE AND GUIDE OTHERS TO YOU.

AUGUST 27

*Each one of us needs to look
after the good of the people around us,
asking ourselves, "How can I help?"*
ROMANS 15:2 THE MESSAGE

All around us are people who have needs, some of which God will call us to help meet. We won't have the strength to do so if we don't depend on Jesus, the One who has both experienced human need and supplied it. Jesus lived to love and serve, and He will give us what we need to do the same for "the good of the people around us" and for His glory. All glory to *Him who is the same*—yesterday, today, and forever!

FATHER, OPEN MY EYES TO THE PEOPLE
AROUND ME WHO HAVE NEEDS THAT
YOU WANT ME TO HELP MEET.
THEN PLEASE STRENGTHEN MY HEART
TO SERVE THEM WITH YOUR LOVE.

AUGUST 28

Love suffers long and is kind.
I CORINTHIANS 13:4 NKJV

Love doesn't give up and stop loving when life gets tough, when days get long, or when someone makes it difficult to respond with love. Love remains patient and calm; love reacts kindly. If we can't do what love would do—if we can't be patient and kind—we need to walk away and until we *can*. God will faithfully, refreshingly, *lovingly* enable us to be patient and kind. And the more times we get it right, the fewer times we'll need to walk away.

FATHER, HELP ME BE ALL THAT LOVE IS—
PATIENT AND KIND,
BUT NOT ENVIOUS, PRIDEFUL,
RUDE, SELF-CENTERED, IRRITABLE—
TO THE PEOPLE IN MY LIFE AND
TO THOSE YOU BRING ACROSS MY PATH.

AUGUST 29

Real wisdom, God's wisdom...
is characterized by getting along with others.
It is gentle and reasonable,
overflowing with mercy and blessings.
JAMES 3:17 THE MESSAGE

We need God's wisdom to love *well*. Wisdom is defined as "experience and knowledge together with the power of applying them." We know where the *power* to live out God's love comes from, but we gain *experience* in loving others only by *practicing it*. We will stumble as we practice, but we can know to pick ourselves up, let God dust us off, and keep practicing. After all, God's love *never* fails.

FATHER, YOU ARE LOVE. PLEASE HELP ME REFLECT YOUR LOVE BY ENABLING ME TO BE KIND, TO NOT ENVY, AND TO NOT BEHAVE RUDELY.

AUGUST 30

Whatever you do,
do it all for the glory of God.
I CORINTHIANS 10:31 NLT

Everything we do with love is an act that gives glory to God. Love is who God is; love is the essence of our heavenly Father. And love is at the heart of God's two greatest commandments: *Love God* and *love others*. When we harness God's power and we are able to love Him and to love others, our lives will shine brightly for His glory.

FATHER, I DESIRE TO DO YOUR WILL, AND YOUR WILL FOR YOUR CHILDREN IS TO LOVE. SO PLEASE LET MY LIFE BE ALL ABOUT LOVE. MAY ALL I DO BRING YOU GLORY.

AUGUST 31

*Every spiritual gift and power
for doing His will are yours.*
I CORINTHIANS 1:7

God's love is *perfect*—and we're *not*. That may be one reason God doesn't ask us to love alone. He knows we are going to mess up, get it wrong, and have to depend on grace *every* day. Thankfully, God's grace—His unmerited favor—will be there in abundance. He will pick us up each time we fall God isn't *ever* going to give up on us; His love will *never* fail.

FATHER, I ASK YOU TO—EACH DAY— GRACIOUSLY GIVE ME A HEART TO LOVE OTHERS THE WAY YOU LOVE ME.

SEPTEMBER 1

Get out there and walk—better yet, run!—
on the road God called you to travel...
pouring yourselves out for each other
in acts of love.
EPHESIANS 4:1-2 THE MESSAGE

Let loving God and loving people be the purpose of your day and the focus of your energy. Choose to be kind in every situation, even—or perhaps especially—in the challenging ones. Keep your eyes open for chances to help someone, and be brave when you realize God has orchestrated for you a "meeting" with someone who has a heart that's searching for His. Respond with God's love: it is the power that brings light to the world, and God wants to shine through you!

FATHER, LET YOUR LOVE POUR
THROUGH ME IN WAYS THAT SHOW
KINDNESS, COMPASSION,
AND A SENSITIVE, CARING HEART.

SEPTEMBER 2

Christ's love controls us now.
II CORINTHIANS 5:14

Jesus came to reveal the love that would change everything by first changing *us*. Now, if there's hope to change the world, it's in our surrendering to God's love *every day*. His love is perfect, and it perfectly guides how we are to act at all times. Specifically, God's love is patient, kind, generous, good, and forgiving If we let that love control us, what a different world it would be!

FATHER, TEACH ME TO LOVE OTHERS BETTER BY LEARNING TO LOVE YOU MORE. I WANT TO HAVE YOUR LOVE CONTROL ME.

SEPTEMBER 3

Love does no wrong to anyone.
ROMANS 13:10

We human beings make mistakes, but love *doesn't*. A loving response is always the right one, forgiving is always the right step forward, and being kind is always the right way to treat people. We're going to have good reasons to ask hard questions about the sad things that happen in the world. But love is never going to be the question *why*. *Love is always going to be the answer.*

FATHER, GIVE ME GRACE TO LOVE MORE, TO DO "NO WRONG TO ANYONE," AND TO BRING THE LIGHT OF YOUR LOVE INTO THIS HURTING WORLD MORE FERVENTLY AND FAITHFULLY.

SEPTEMBER 4

*May our dependably steady and warmly
personal God develop maturity in you
so that you get along with each other.*
ROMANS 15:5-6 THE MESSAGE

We serve an up-close-and-personal God.
More than anything else, He wants us to
love *Him and to love each other*. He gives
us His love to share from His unlimited
supply so that, by the power of His Spirit
within us, we are able to love as He did—
selflessly and sacrificially. So let's lean on
our "dependably steady" Father today
and love the people around us *His* way!

FATHER, I WANT TO KNOW YOU BETTER
AND DEPEND ON YOU MORE, SO I CAN
LOVE OTHERS MORE LIKE YOU DO.

SEPTEMBER 5

Give all your worries and cares to God,
for He cares for you.
I PETER 5:7 NLT

If we're going to let love and kindness *rule more*, we're going to have to *carry less*— less concern about getting everything done and less fretting about whether or not we're getting everything right. Giving all our "worries and cares to God" is as simple as giving Him the reins every day. We hesitate, but we don't need to. Today's verse tells us He cares; it reminds us that He's got us! And He's got us right where He wants us to be, where we are able to love the ones who need that love most.

FATHER, THANK YOU THAT YOU DO CARE FOR ME AND ABOUT ME. PLEASE USE ME IN THE PLACE YOU HAVE ME, ENABLING ME TO TREAT OTHERS WITH KINDNESS AND LOVE.

SEPTEMBER 6

When I pray,
You answer me and encourage me
by giving me the strength I need.

PSALM 138:3

God's love for us whom He created and who have named His Son, Jesus, as our Savior and Lord is strong. Nothing can ever separate us from God's love, and God asks us to love others, but not with any power of our own. We won't last long if we're relying on our own strength. But God will give us the strength we need, and that *strength is only a prayer away*.

FATHER, GIVE ME YOUR JOY AND STRENGTH AS I SHARE YOUR LOVE WITH OTHERS TODAY.

SEPTEMBER 7

*All praise to God
for His wonderful kindness to us.*
EPHESIANS 1:6

What if we began each day by praising God for "His wonderful kindness," His amazing grace, and His unconditional love that models for us how to love others. We don't need to wait for a reason to love, and may we not expect a certain response or any kind of reward for doing it. May we love simply because God first loved us. Similarly, let us be kind because God has shown His wonderful kindness to us. He's the only *why'* we need...and love's the only way we'll change this world.

FATHER, I PRAISE YOU FOR YOUR WONDERFUL KINDNESS AND PERFECT LOVE. MAY EVEN MY MEAGER ACTS OF KINDNESS AND LOVE SHINE YOUR LIGHT INTO THE WORLD.

SEPTEMBER 8

This is what I have asked God for you:
that you will be encouraged and knit together
by strong ties of love.
COLOSSIANS 2:2

Love brings us together. Love makes every person feel valued. It means kindness, empathy, and *unity*. Love enables us to look past and even to push aside our differences. In other words, love helps us see how alike we are. Each one of us was created by an awesome God, and given a unique set of gifts, so that we can *be blessings to each other*.

FATHER, SHOW ME WAYS I CAN BE A
BLESSING BY SHARING YOUR LOVE,
KINDNESS, AND COMPASSION.

SEPTEMBER 9

God who began the good work within you
will keep right on helping you
grow in His grace.

PHILIPPIANS 1:6

For God's love to grow in the world, our love for Him has to grow *our hearts*. When we give our lives to Him, His love comes in to transform us. We will never exhaust the transformative power of God's love, nor will we completely grasp the fullness of God's love for us. Yet our hearts *can* come to hold *more* and then to share *more* of God's love as we put our trust in Him *more* and *more*.

FATHER, AS YOUR LOVE CONTINUES TO TRANSFORM MY HEART, PLEASE HELP ME ACT ON MY EVER-GROWING DESIRE TO SHARE YOUR LOVE WITH OTHERS.

SEPTEMBER 10

Mark me with Your sign of love.
Plan only the best for me, GOD!
PSALM 25:7 THE MESSAGE

We have the privilege of being living sign-posts for God's love. *Here is God's amazing love! This is what it looks like!* Every day is a new beginning, and every day is filled with opportunities to bring to earth a little bit of heaven. We have the privilege to touching people's lives with the peace, joy, and light of God as well as—most important—*His miraculous love.* He has nothing less than the *best* He for us... *and for every person whose life we touch.*

FATHER, YOUR LOVE CHANGES
EVERYTHING: YOUR LOVE BRINGS
THE BEST AND MOST BEAUTIFUL
THINGS TO LIFE.

SEPTEMBER 11

Everything we know about God's word
is summed up in a single sentence:
Love others as you love yourself.
GALATIANS 5:14 THE MESSAGE

The sum of all the reasons we're here on this earth is to *love*. We are first and foremost to love God, but—as Paul wrote in Galatians 5:14—we are to love others as we love ourselves. This kind of outward-looking, selfless love brings the best possible outcome to *every interaction* we have on this earth. Love also leads others to the life of forgiveness and joy God offers. When they accept, they discover *their* purpose—which is to love! What a beautiful dance to be part of!

> FATHER, YOUR LOVE CAPTURES HEARTS AND CHANGES LIVES. LET ME BE ONE WHO FULLY SHARES THAT MESSAGE WITH MY WORDS AND ACTIONS—AND FOR YOUR GLORY.

SEPTEMBER 12

Share each other's troubles and problems,
and so obey our Lord's command.
GALATIANS 6:2

Most of us learned to share when we were children, and our heavenly Father wants us to share as grown-ups too. Now, however, we are sharing much different things than we were early in our lives. We are, for instance, to the troubles and problems that all of us experience. None of us escapes sufferings. But people who love us are willing to come alongside and share the weight of the heartache. May we do the same when we see someone hurting.

FATHER, GIVE ME A HEART FULL OF COMPASSION, WILLING TO SHARE THE BURDENS I SEE PEOPLE CARRYING.

SEPTEMBER 13

Let love be your greatest aim.
I CORINTHIANS 14:1

Love *loves* to give,
And it's quick to do
Whatever is needed
To help you get through.
When life takes a down,
Instead of an up,
You'd see it half full
If you just had a cup!
Love rushes in
Without flinching or pause,
To rescue the day—
But, please, no applause.
Love needs no kudos,
No stage or spotlight;
Love serves its neighbor
So more love *ignites*.

> FATHER, LET ME BE YOUR LOVE TO AS
> MANY AS I CAN, AS OFTEN AS I CAN,
> AND WITH JOY WHEREVER YOU LEAD!

━━━ ❧ ━━━

SEPTEMBER 14

Keep on loving others.
HEBREWS 6:11 NLT

If we love God, loving others isn't an option. Love should be coursing through our spiritual veins to the point of *influencing everything we say and do*. We aren't going to reach perfection, but we can reach out to other people for *Him*—sharing His strength, wisdom, longsuffering, kindness, and patience—*every single day*. Relying on the Spirit to do so is going to make us more and more like Him in *every way*.

FATHER, MY DESIRE IS TO LOVE OTHERS THE WAY THAT YOU LOVE ME. MAKE MY HEART MORE LIKE YOURS— MORE GENEROUS, PATIENT, AND KIND.

SEPTEMBER 15

I love You, LORD;
You are my strength.
PSALM 18:1 NLT

God's strength in our weakness is one of His greatest gifts to those who love Him. It means, among other things, that we don't have to do life alone *ever*. Why would we want to when the Creator of the universe is standing at the ready? His outstretched hand waits for us to take hold in our moment of need. When we do, He'll not only lift us out of all fear, uncertainty, and weakness, but He'll replace it with faith, confidence, and strength.

FATHER, YOU ARE MY HOPE AND MY
PROVISION FOR EVERY NEED.
TEACH ME TO TRUST YOU
WITH ALL MY HEART!

SEPTEMBER 16

The godly love to give!
PROVERBS 21:26 NLT

The heart that loves God becomes more *like* God—*and He loves to give*. It's not a matter of whether or not we *have* something to give: God is all-sufficient and, by the power of His Spirit living within His children, God is *our Source* for whatever He calls us to share. So when the door opens to reflect His love, or when He *opens our eyes* to a need we can meet because He has blessed us, may we happily serve one another because we *faithfully* serve Him.

FATHER, YOUR LIFE-CHANGING LOVE
COMPELS ME TO LOVE AND
SERVE OTHERS WITH A WILLING,
HAPPY HEART!

SEPTEMBER 17

Love does not demand its own way.

I CORINTHIANS 13:5

We all like to have our own way. It's part of the ongoing battle between our flesh and our spirit. The beautiful truth is that we can win every time if we choose love at every turn. No matter how we feel or how many reasons we could come up with for choosing anything less than love, our surrendering to God's love keeps us from demanding our way over serving another with love.

FATHER, YOU GIVE YOUR LOVE FREELY AND UNCONDITIONALLY.
PLEASE STRENGTHEN MY SPIRIT SO I WILL LOVE LIKE YOU LOVE:
FREELY AND UNCONDITIONALLY.

SEPTEMBER 18

*Be gentle and
show true humility to everyone.*
TITUS 3:2 NLT

Only rarely do we not feel rushed as we move through our days, so it isn't always easy to respond to others with gentleness and humility. But God's love is always there to enable us to love. God never expects us to go it alone: He helps us first to choose to do good and to love others and then to act on that choice. Our heavenly Father knows we need Him to help us love, and He's always faithful to do so.

FATHER, GIVE ME THE FULLNESS OF
YOUR SPIRIT AND STRENGTH SO THAT
I CAN LOVE OTHERS WHEN I'M EMPTY.

SEPTEMBER 19

*God loves you and has chosen you
to be His own people.*
I THESSALONIANS 1:4 NLT

Whenever you're challenged, over-whelmed, or defeated, remember you're chosen. God called you to do things that require you to *completely* depend on Him. Apart from Him—*completely* independent of God—none of us can love the way God wants us to love. Love in all its fullness is found in Him, and the more we savor His love for us, the more easily we give that love to others.

FATHER, THANK YOU FOR CHOOSING ME, FOR LOVING ME FAITHFULLY, AND FOR ENABLING ME TO LOVE OTHERS.

SEPTEMBER 20

You are precious to Me.
You are honored, and I love you.
ISAIAH 43:4 NLT

It's a simple and beautiful picture of God's love: He counts us precious simply because we are His children. We never have to—we never even could—earn His love. We receive what He offers and, as a result, can always feel valued, accepted, and loved *no matter what*. Love is the reason God brings people together—and it's the most important gift we'll ever give to each other.

FATHER, LET THE BEAUTY OF YOUR
CONSTANT LOVE FILL ME WITH THE
DESIRE TO SHOW IT TO OTHERS WITH
A WILLING AND OPEN HEART.

SEPTEMBER 21

Give generously... not grudgingly,
*for the L*ORD *your God will bless you*
in everything you do.
DEUTERONOMY 15:10 NLT

Let's be generous—as God is—with love.
Loving people may cost us a little time as
we take a few moments to put the needs
of others before our own. After all, love
holds the power to ease life's difficulties.
God sees hungering hearts and knows His
love can satisfy them. That's one reason
He blessings those who live to give it.

FATHER, GIVE ME A FULL AND
GENEROUS HEART. I WANT TO BE A
CHANNEL OF YOUR LOVE EVERY DAY.

SEPTEMBER 22

How kind the Lord is!
How good He is!
PSALM 116:5 NLT

Our kindness is a little drop of God's love in the world—and, by His power and grace, a little goes a long way! Someone's day can be changed by your kind words or actions. A person who hasn't felt loved in a while can be reminded that *God sees* them...and hasn't left them. Someone else might need a bright spot in the day to have the courage to go on. God knows the need—and uses us to bring the love!

FATHER, GIVE ME OPEN EYES AND A KIND HEART SO THAT I WILL SEIZE EVERY OPPORTUNITY TO ADD SOME OF YOUR LOVE AND GOODNESS TO THE WORLD.

SEPTEMBER 23

Three things will last forever—
faith, hope, and love—
and the greatest of these is love.
I CORINTHIANS 13:13 NLT

Love makes everything better because love is the *greatest thing ever*! God's love is the greatest gift, the highest purpose, the sweetest reflection of His heart—and here we are in this great big world with the privilege of sharing it. Our lives send messages and pictures of His love every day. Let's make them as true and clear as we can by staying close and connected to Him.

FATHER, THANK YOU FOR CHOOSING
ME TO SHOW OFF YOUR LOVE,
THE MOST BEAUTIFUL PART OF YOU.
PLEASE HELP ME BE FAITHFUL
TO LOVE OTHERS FULLY.

SEPTEMBER 24

*Remember me in the light
of Your unfailing love.*

PSALM 25:7 NLT

The light of God's love brightens our lives so that people are drawn to Him. Every day is another chance for us to shine. And God's love shines in a favor for no reason... a willingness to smile first...a thoughtful action...a kind word...a text to say, "I'm thinking about you"... and a few minutes to do that little thing God has put on your heart to do—that He knows will make someone feel His love in a *big* way.

FATHER, HELP ME TO BE FAITHFUL AND SHINE YOUR LOVE BRIGHTLY TODAY!

SEPTEMBER 25

This is my command:
Love each other.
JOHN 15:17 NLT

These are six of the simplest yet *most significant* words Jesus spoke. He is very straightforward with this command to love. He wants us to be in the place where His love is in control of our hearts—which means *He's* in control. You and I can't be more blessed than when we're in the place of completely trusting Him, reflected in our compassionate and generous love for others.

FATHER, LET ME ALWAYS HAVE
THE DESIRE TO LOVE YOU MORE
COMPLETELY SO THAT I CAN LOVE
OTHERS BETTER.

Don't be anxious about tomorrow.
God will take care of your tomorrow too.
Live one day at a time.
MATTHEW 6:34

Worry washes away our ability to love. If can't live in the moment, we can't love with our whole hearts. So let's remember that God's got our day handled and our tomorrow covered! Also, He's going to put someone *right in front* of us who needs His love *right now*. When we trust God to take care of our cares, we free our hearts to love others in the *best way*.

FATHER, YOU ARE MY PEACE
AND MY PROVISION. PLEASE GIVE ME
THE COURAGE I NEED TO GIVE
YOU EVERY CARE SO I CAN LOVE
OTHERS COMPLETELY.

SEPTEMBER 27

*A branch can't produce fruit
when severed from the vine.
Nor can you be fruitful apart from Me.*

JOHN 15:4

Our lives are in Jesus when we have named Him our Savior and Lord—and our lives are all about loving others with the love we get from *His life within* us. We can't produce the fruit that makes an eternal difference if we don't fill our hearts with His eternal love. And we want everything we do to grow *everlasting* fruit from *love that never fails*. So let's stay connected to God, be courageous, and count on Him to use us as He brings forth a beautiful harvest of love.

FATHER, I SURRENDER MY WHOLE
HEART TO YOU, SO THAT MY LIFE AND
THE LOVE I GIVE WILL BE FRUITFUL.

SEPTEMBER 28

*Make the most of every opportunity
you have for doing good.*
EPHESIANS 5:16

Seizing every opportunity to do good means jumping at every chance you have to experience *real joy*. God knows what our hearts need to be fulfilled and to stay filled with His blessings—*and they all begin with love*. Every time we give love, we experience God's love. That path of walking in God's love and loving others leads to the best life, the biggest rewards, and the brightest joy.

FATHER, I ASK YOU TO HELP ME SEE
AND SEIZE EVERY CHANCE TO DO
SOMETHING GOOD AND THEREBY
OFFER PEOPLE A PICTURE OF
YOUR LOVE.

SEPTEMBER 29

*Take tender care of those who are weak,
and be patient with everyone.*
I THESSALONIANS 5:14

There's no way for us to know how battle-weakened people are when we first meet them. And that's one reason why their treatment of us should never determine our treatment of them. Instead, let's pray to be patient, especially with those who clearly need a touch of God's love and tenderness. Life is a difficult road, and sometimes God brings the strong alongside the weak to bless them with His love.

FATHER, GIVE ME A PATIENT, CARING HEART, THE ABILITY TO SEE THE NEEDS OF PEOPLE AROUND ME, AND YOUR LOVE TO GIVE TO THOSE WHO ARE HURTING.

SEPTEMBER 30

*If you think you are too important
to help someone, you are only fooling yourself.
You are not that important.*
GALATIANS 6:3 NLT

Sometimes we need this stark reminder:
God does not deem a single person on
this planet more important than another.
*Every single person throughout all time
cost God the life of His Son.* We're here to
help each other, to learn to love Him completely and to love others unconditionally.
When we see a need, let's listen closely
so we can clearly hear, "This is how you
can help."

FATHER, MAKE ME A HUMBLE SERVANT
WHO LOVES WITHOUT CONDITION AND
HELPS WITHOUT RESERVATION.

OCTOBER 1

He'll calm you with His love.
ZEPHANIAH 3:17 THE MESSAGE

Love is patient. It's all too easy to answer harshly and quickly especially when an intense situation is escalating. But our God is slow to anger, and He can help us be like that too. When we let love stay in control, it keeps our emotions under control. What grace, that God' *faithfully quiets us with His love...so He can quicken our spirits to act the way the One who is love acts.*

FATHER, CALM ME WITH YOUR LOVE TODAY. THEN PLEASE HELP ME BE PATIENT, KIND, AND LOVING TOWARD THE PEOPLE I ENCOUNTER AS WELL AS THOSE I LIVE WITH.

OCTOBER 2

Each day the Lᴏʀᴅ pours
His unfailing love upon me.
PSALM 42:8 NLT

We start every day loved by God from head to toe. Not a moment of any day passes without His love, no worries can stand against it, and not a thing can come between heaven's waterfall of love and us. God pours it on and we stand beneath the blessings it brings! Open your heart and let them come—peace for whatever has you anxious, hope for whatever has you waiting, and courage for whatever comes your way.

FATHER, THANK YOU FOR CONTINUOUSLY POURING YOUR LOVE INTO MY LIFE—AND FOR EVERY GOOD THING THAT COMES WHEN I EMBRACE IT AND SHARE IT!

OCTOBER 3

God doesn't miss anything.
He knows perfectly well
all the love you've shown...
and that you keep at it.
HEBREWS 6:10 THE MESSAGE

Everything we do with a spirit of love makes God smile. After all, love changes hearts, and in the moment God's love is shared, people get a glimpse of *Him*. He's the Source of every good thing in our lives, and His love is the greatest thing we'll ever give *or* receive. Remembering that God's love enables us to shine, consider what you might do to keep your life lighting the way to Him

FATHER, YOUR LOVE SHEDS LIGHT ON
YOUR BEAUTY. I ASK YOU TO FILL ME
WITH THE JOY OF SHINING YOUR LOVE
ON EVERY LIFE I TOUCH.

OCTOBER 4

As we obey this commandment,
to love one another, the darkness
in our lives disappears and
the new light of life in Christ shines in.

I JOHN 2:8

What an amazing, *miraculous* power God's love is! His love opens the door to our hearts to His truth, allowing the light of Christ to shine in. When our hearts are filled with His love, our lives become flashlights—or perhaps sometimes flood-lights—to people around us. Every time we're kind, thoughtful, forgiving, compassionate, or understanding, the world gets a *brighter* and *better* view of our great and gracious God!

FATHER, GIVE ME A HEART TO LOVE
OTHERS UNCONDITIONALLY
SO THEY SEE YOUR LIGHT IN ME.

OCTOBER 5

*Let everyone see that you are unselfish
and considerate in all you do.*
PHILIPPIANS 4:5

God puts the light of His love *within* us
while the world puts a spotlight on *what
we do*. When we trust God to guide us,
we allow His love to govern us, and the
more often love becomes a part of *all we
do*. Leading a selfless and considerate life
doesn't come by chance, though. It comes
when we choose love!

FATHER, I TRUST YOU TO GROW A DEEP
AND DELIBERATE LOVE IN ME,
ONE THAT LEADS ME TO BE SELFLESS
AND KIND IN ALL I DO.

OCTOBER 6

*Give me understanding and
I will obey Your instructions; I will put them
into practice with all my heart.*

PSALM 119:34 NLT

God gives us a simple instruction for living: *love one another.* Simple to understand, but not easy to put into practice. The cares of life and any stress and fear they cause can disrupt our life-giving and love-giving connection with God and hinder us from both doing what love does and reflecting what love is. So we need to *"give all [our] worries and cares to God, for He cares about [us]"* (I Peter 5:7 NLT). We need to let go in order to let love flow—*from His heart...through ours... to others.*

FATHER, I LAY ALL MY WORRIES AND
CARES AT YOUR FEET, SO MY HEART
CAN BE FILLED WITH YOUR LOVE AND
THEN I CAN BE FREE TO GIVE IT.

OCTOBER 7

An understanding person remains calm.
PROVERBS 17:27 THE MESSAGE

We need to completely depend on God if we're going to love others completely. We're too often tired, rushed, overwhelmed, and tempted to distraction by scrolling screens. In sharp contrast, God is strong, peaceful, sufficient, and *always focused on us*. He's the Source for our every need and our Example for *everything love is*. When we rest in Him and rely on His grace, we can enjoy as well as *extend* the calmness of His love.

FATHER, I ASK YOU TO GIVE ME THE GRACE TO LOVE OTHERS WITH A CALM HEART THAT IS COMPLETELY COMMITTED TO YOU.

OCTOBER 8

Observe how Christ loved us.
His love was not cautious but extravagant.
EPHESIANS 5:2 THE MESSAGE

Perfectly and powerfully. Unconditionally and unyieldingly. Extravagantly and eternally. That's how Christ loves us! May His love inspire us to love others when it's hard to do, when they don't love us in return, and when our hearts get broken and we worry that they'll *never* go back together again. Jesus' love reminds us again and again, *I am here... I am wholeness... and I am always and forever everything you need*.

FATHER, I WANT TO FULLY LEAN ON YOU AND LOOK TO YOUR LOVE FOR EVERYTHING MY HEART NEEDS SO I AM ABLE TO LOVE OTHERS WELL.

OCTOBER 9

I am always aware of Your unfailing love.
PSALM 26:3 NLT

The world's design—the goal of the enemy of our souls—is to distract us from what's important by making us think the temporal is permanent. The *only thing* in life that's urgent is also *unfailing*, *indestructible*, and *unending*—and that is God's love! To always be aware of its presence and power, we have to make spending time with Him a priority. Love is time well spent, the best investment, and it's the one thing that makes life worthwhile.

FATHER, I LONG TO HAVE A HEART
THAT'S ALWAYS AWARE OF YOUR LOVE
AND OF THE AMAZING PRIVILEGE
OF SHARING YOUR LOVE
WITH THE WORLD.

OCTOBER 10

*Turn both your pockets and
our hearts inside out and give generously.*
LUKE 11:41 THE MESSAGE

With God as the infinite Source of love, we need never run low on love, so let's open our hearts and give, give, GIVE! When we do, we will know the blessings of genuine joy... true contentment... a heavenly Father who's pleased... and the most fulfilling life we can imagine. Gaining things isn't the thing that life is all about. It never was, and it never will be. *Love is the thing*—the one and only thing—that means *everything*.

FATHER, FILL ME WITH YOUR LIFE AND
YOUR LOVE, SO THAT MY LIFE WILL
MIRROR ALL THAT TRULY MATTERS—
YOU AND YOUR LOVE.

OCTOBER 11

*What you say flows from
what is in your heart.*
LUKE 6:45 NLT

Words matter. Alive and powerful, they are able to *build up or break down*. That's why it's vital to stay prayerful, close to God, and full of His love. Consider your heart the holding tank for what will fuel your words. What we say will either promote love or perpetuate hate, either be filled with grace or burdened by negativity. Let's *let God's love fill our hearts and then guide our words*.

FATHER, FILL ME WITH YOUR WISDOM
AND LOVE, I ASK, AND THEN MAY YOUR
SPIRIT GUIDE MY WORDS.

OCTOBER 12

*Morning by morning He wakens me
and opens my understanding to His will.*
ISAIAH 50:4 NLT

God's perfect will for our lives is to *love*. We don't have to search and wonder or wait and see what God wants us to do with the days and years He's given us. He wants us to *love*. If we trust God completely, we will allow His love to guide us. The place we are now and the people we're with now are all a part of His plan to *teach us about His love*—because we can't do *eternal things* until we understand love is *everything*.

FATHER, PLEASE HELP ME BE CONTENT
AND CONFIDENT IN YOUR WILL,
KNOWING THAT RIGHT WHERE I AM,
I CAN LEARN TO LOVE YOU MORE.

OCTOBER 13

*We know how dearly God loves us,
and we feel this warm love everywhere
within us because God has given us
the Holy Spirit to fill our lives with His love.*

ROMANS 5:5

When we put love into practice, our hearts are close to God, and that's a place of *pure* joy! In fact, loving people is the best way to spread the most joy and make the biggest difference in a world that desperately needs Him. God's love brings light, lifts sadness, lightens cares, and leads to life everlasting. By the power of God's Holy Spirit, His goodness lies within us—always ready for Him to use to change the world around us.

FATHER, THANK YOU FOR FILLING OUR
HEARTS WITH YOUR LOVE—
AND FOR GIVING US THE POWER OF
YOUR SPIRIT TO SHARE IT.

OCTOBER 14

*The person who truly loves God is the one
who is open to God's knowledge.*

I CORINTHIANS 8:3

God wants us to be lifelong learners about
His love and His grace. We'll never exhaust
His supply of either one, and this side of
heaven we'll never get to the point finally
being able to love others like He does. But
we *can* keep our hearts open and our spirits humble when He reveals areas we need
to grow in. Such God-directed growth can
of course help us get better at loving others and therefore better reflect God's love
to those around us.

FATHER, I WANT TO KNOW YOU MORE
SO OTHERS CAN SEE MORE OF YOUR
LOVE IN ME.

OCTOBER 15

*Love is... never jealous or envious...
never haughty or selfish or rude.*
I CORINTHIANS 13:4-5

The list of things *love never does* may include some of the very things we stumble over. When too few things go smoothly and too many things go wrong; when our feelings get run over and our hearts get hurt; and when everyone and everything is challenging us, we find it tough to make it through a day. Thankfully, God never expects perfection. Instead, He promises never-ending peace—and all the grace you'll ever need.

FATHER, THANK YOU FOR YOUR
FAITHFUL LOVE... AND FOR REFRESHING
MY SPIRIT WITH YOUR GRACE
AND YOUR PEACE.

OCTOBER 16

Most of all, love each other
as if your life depended on it.
Love makes up for practically anything.
I PETER 4:8 THE MESSAGE

Love is the greatest gift in life! It's a one-word description of our all-powerful God, and love makes *all* the difference in our time on this earth. We are wise to choose to spend our time loving others even if we leave a lot of things undone that really don't matter a whole lot. Love holds us together and keeps us connected to God—and that's what enriches *every* life.

FATHER, YOU ARE LOVE, AND YOU ARE THE GIVER OF LIFE. MAKE MY LIFE A CHANNEL OF EVERY GOOD GIFT THAT COMES FROM YOU.

OCTOBER 17

Be tenderhearted,
and keep a humble attitude.
I PETER 3:8 NLT

When life keeps us tangled up in temporal things, we can lose sight of the eternal things—and those are the ones that matter. *Relationship* is why we're here. *Love* is why we're here. Love brings our priorities into focus because it puts our focus on God. Humility and gentleness are the ways we live out love and goodness—and doing so should *always* be our heart's desire.

FATHER, GIVE ME A TENDER HEART AND
A HUMBLE SPIRIT, SO THAT MY LIFE
WILL POINT OTHERS TO YOU.

OCTOBER 18

*Let us think of ways
to motivate one another to acts of love
and good works.*
HEBREWS 10:24 NLT

Maybe the best way to run a lifelong marathon of love is to recognize that the starting line is squarely in front of us every morning. When we awaken, let us choose a good attitude and a focus on our great God. May we let Him set the course for our day and not worry if our schedule gets sidetracked. Let's *be* the love that *spreads* the love in a world that desperately *needs His love!*

FATHER, LET MY HEART BE MOTIVATED
TO GIVE LOVE AND TO DO GOOD SO
THE WORLD CAN SEE MORE OF YOU.

OCTOBER 19

*God has not given us a spirit
of fear and timidity,
but of power, love, and self-discipline.*
II TIMOTHY 1:7 NLT

God's love is strong, confident, and powerful. God has given us the Holy Spirit to lead us in the way of His love as we surrender our hearts to God and make the commitment to follow Him. When God asks us to meet someone's need, extend a kindness, or show His love through a simple gesture, we can be confident there's a greater purpose we can't see—and we should be willing to follow through.

FATHER, HELP ME BE SENSITIVE TO
YOUR SPIRIT'S LEADING AND FAITHFUL
AND BOLD IN SHARING YOUR LOVE.

OCTOBER 20

*May the Lord lead your hearts
into a full understanding and
expression of the love of God.*

II THESSALONIANS 3:5 NLT

If our hearts could *fully express* God's love, we'd run out of days before we'd run out of ways! His kindnesses to us outnumber the stars in the sky, and the goodness of His grace is greater than *anything* this world offers. The more we meditate on and live in His love, the more we'll want to *give it* and *live it*.

FATHER, LEAD MY HEART TO KNOW
YOUR LOVE MORE FULLY AND TO GIVE
IT MORE FREELY.

OCTOBER 21

*Love each other deeply
with all your heart.*
I PETER 1:22 NLT

Dig deep and love large. Show God's love everywhere you go and every chance you get! Then you may feel a burst of joy every time you open your heart and let love out. Also, loving others doesn't deplete our energy; it energizes our spirit and ignites our purpose. And good things become great things when we do them with a genuine, generous, godly love.

FATHER, FILL MY LIFE WITH THE JOY
OF LOVING OTHERS AS MY HEART
REJOICES IN LOVING AND BEING
LOVED BY YOU!

OCTOBER 22

*Pursue righteous living,
faithfulness, love, and peace.*
II TIMOTHY 2:22 NLT

Love is always the right thing to do. We need to let it influence our responses and be the reason we treat others with kindness and respect. Love brings God into the center of any situation, and His presence brings the best possible outcome. It's tough to argue with kindness and impossible to defeat love, so may we animate love with our actions!

FATHER, GIVE ME A HEART THAT'S FAITHFUL TO YOU AND FILLED WITH YOUR LOVE.

OCTOBER 23

*You can't go wrong
when you love others.*
ROMANS 13:10 THE MESSAGE

Love is *always* right. How we share it doesn't matter—and there are *endless* ways to show God's love and *zero* ways of getting it wrong! Love is patient, kind, caring, compassionate, generous, encouraging, peaceful, forgiving, and the *best thing we can do* to grow in grace. And what is the best reason to grow in grace? So we can give even *more* love.

FATHER, YOUR LOVE MAKES THE
WORLD BEAUTIFUL AND LIFE
MEANINGFUL. GIVE ME A HEART
TO GIVE IT MORE FAITHFULLY.

OCTOBER 24

Love does no wrong to anyone.
ROMANS 13:10

Love is *incredibly* kind. It is *incapable* of mistreating others. If only we could always rise above our moods and *never* do wrong to anyone. But we do hurt people. And when we do, we are to rely on God's grace to forgive us and to move us forward—at the same time that we trust *His* perfect love to heal the hearts that we have hurt. He will be faithful to restore... and we'll grow in grace a little more.

FATHER, I WANT TO WALK IN LOVE AND GROW IN GRACE SO THAT OTHERS SEE MORE OF YOUR PERFECT LOVE REFLECTED IN ME.

OCTOBER 25

Keep company with [God]
and learn a life of love.
EPHESIANS 5:2 THE MESSAGE

A life of love takes a lot of *leaning on* and *learning from* God. He teaches us to love by giving us opportunities to love the people He brings into our lives and the circumstances He allows. If we pay attention, pray, and keep our hearts open to self-reflection and *correction*, we will continue to grow in our capacity to love Him and to love others.

FATHER, TEACH ME TO BE SENSITIVE
TO YOUR SPIRIT AND WILLING TO
GROW BETTER AT LOVING YOU
AND OTHERS.

OCTOBER 26

Let love be your highest goal!
I CORINTHIANS 14:1 NLT

If we're going to live the *best life* we can possibly live, we need to focus on love! *People*—not position, promotion, or possessions—*matter most.* God wired us to need each other and, in dependence on Him, to love each other. God is love, and He created us to help each other along life's journey. Love truly is to be our highest goal.

FATHER, HELP ME SEE THE NEEDS OF THE PEOPLE AROUND ME AND HUMBLY SERVE THEM WITH YOUR LOVE AND GRACE.

OCTOBER 27

No good thing will He withhold
from those who walk along His paths.

PSALM 84:11

Love is a good thing—and God will not do *anything* to withhold it from our lives. His love is here to guide us and help us. His love enables us to love others without hesitation, judgment, or fear. We can be bold and brave with His love that breaks every chain of inferiority, discouragement, and doubt. The power and *privilege* to love others is ours today, so let's be God's love in *every* way!

FATHER, THANK YOU FOR EVERY GOOD GIFT IN MY LIFE AND FOR EVERY GOOD GIFT YOU GIVE THROUGH MY LIFE BY THE POWER OF YOUR LOVE.

OCTOBER 28

When others are happy, be happy with them.
If they are sad, share their sorrow.
ROMANS 12:15

Empathy is one of love's most beautiful qualities. God asks us to share each other's joy and sadness alike because one element of love is *sharing*. Being present for another can bring comfort. Being together can bring healing. God wants *us all* to remember that we are not alone. In the storms and in the celebrations, let's stay connected by one of the things that makes us alike—*our need for love.*

FATHER, LET ME LOVE WITH EMPATHY,
GRACE, AND A WILLINGNESS
TO BE THERE FOR OTHERS
IN THEIR TIME OF NEED.

OCTOBER 29

You have every grace and blessing;
every spiritual gift and
power for doing His will are yours.

I CORINTHIANS 1:7

Having God's Spirit within us, we have everything we need to cultivate a life of love. His will for our lives is—first and foremost—to *love*, and loving others takes a daily dependence on His strength, patience, forgiveness, and compassion. He blesses us to, in turn, bless others so the gifts of His grace may go on and on.

FATHER, YOU GIVE THE GIFTS WE NEED
TO FILL THE WORLD WITH YOUR LOVE.
THANK YOU FOR YOUR GRACE
AND GOODNESS.

OCTOBER 30

Love each other with genuine affection,
and take delight in honoring each other.

ROMANS 12:10 NLT

Genuine love speaks by doing. It goes out of its way to make someone else's way a little easier. Genuine love is empowered by God alone. If we want to love others without judgment or conditions, we will do so only by trusting God: He is the only One who can teach us to see our fellow human beings with His eyes. Only God can prompt in our hearts genuine affection for others.

FATHER, I WANT TO YIELD TO YOUR LOVE SO YOU CAN CONTINUE TO TRANSFORM MY HEART. I WANT TO DELIGHT IN THE PEOPLE YOU GIVE ME TO LOVE AND BE ABLE TO LOVE THEM WITH GENUINE AFFECTION.

OCTOBER 31

*Life is worth nothing unless I use it for doing
the work assigned me by the Lord Jesus—
the work of telling others the Good News
about God's mighty kindness and love.*

· ACTS 20:24

We can spend our lives making plans, arranging schedules, and keeping appointments, but if we rush around without truly loving others, we won't accomplish anything of lasting worth. Wisdom would tell us not to wait until our last days to reevaluate our life's work. God wants to work at what matters most *right now*. The world is yearning to *know* His love, and He is counting on us to *show* His love.

FATHER, HELP ME PUT YOU FIRST AND
MAKE LOVING YOU AND SHARING YOUR
LOVE MY TOP PRIORITY.

NOVEMBER 1

Lord, through all the generations
You have been our home!
Before the mountains were created,
before the earth was formed,
You are God without beginning or end.

PSALM 90:1-2

God truly is our home. A place where we're known, blessed, and reminded that we're valued and cherished. A place where comfort overflows, sorrows fade, and cares disappear. God never moves away...changes... or becomes difficult to find. He's the same yesterday, today, and forever. And even though we experience constant changes in our lives and in the world, we can go to God *where we find everything arranged with love and securely in place.*

FATHER, YOU ARE MY REFUGE AT ALL TIMES. IN YOU I FIND THE LOVE AND GRACE I NEED TO GO ON.

NOVEMBER 2

When the Holy Spirit controls our lives
He will produce this kind of fruit in us:
love, joy, peace, patience, kindness, goodness,
faithfulness, gentleness and self-control.

GALATIANS 5:22-23

The fruit of the Holy Spirit is a harvest we should all want in our lives! Love is first on the list because when we choose to *love others*, the other fruits follow. And those other fruits—the other characteristics of a Spirit-led life—are examples of how love *acts*. The various fruits of the Spirit fit together beautifully...and living a fruitful life begins with love.

FATHER, HELP ME FINE-TUNE
A SPIRIT-LED LIFE, SO OTHERS
CAN SEE MORE CLEARLY IN ME
A PICTURE OF YOUR LOVE.

NOVEMBER 3

The godly are generous givers.
PSALM 37:21 NLT

The godly are generous givers, the psalmist proclaimed—and we should be *most* generous when it comes to love! We can start a chain reaction of love in the world by our kindness, by our caring, or simply by looking into the eyes of someone as we talk together. Even little things can make a person feel honored and valued—especially in our age when our screens too easily dominate our time and attention.

FATHER, PLEASE ENABLE ME TO GIVE
PRIORITY TO PEOPLE OVER SCREENS.
I WANT TO PAY ATTENTION
TO THE NEEDS AROUND ME AND
THEN SEIZE THE OPPORTUNITIES
TO SHOW YOUR LOVE.

NOVEMBER 4

Mostly what God does is love you.
Keep company with Him
and learn a life of love.
EPHESIANS 5:2 THE MESSAGE

Mostly... love. What a spot-on goal for our lives! Each one of us is in a constant learning process when we're in the company of God, and one lesson every day is love. Nothing else we do matters more because nothing else lasts for eternity. God is love. Loving Him is in itself one of life's *greatest blessings*. God wants *every person* to know His heart—and love is the best way we can show them.

FATHER, YOUR LOVE IS MY HOPE,
MY JOY, MY PEACE, AND MY PURPOSE.
LET ME BE FERVENT IN SHOWING IT
TO OTHERS.

NOVEMBER 5

The Sovereign Lord has given me
His words of wisdom,
so that I know how to comfort the weary.
ISAIAH 50:4 NLT

When we come alongside someone who's hurting and offer comfort, we experience an intimate time with God. That's because He is close to the brokenhearted. He understands pain, rejection, loneliness, loss, and anything else we encounter in this fallen world. And God's desire is to love broken souls back to wholeness in Him. If we ask, He'll guide us as we help a family member or friend through the sorrow. Our faithful God will either give us words to say or the reassurance that silence is good, and He will make His presence known as we sit with the one we care about. God is *faithful*—and we can trust His love *won't fail.*

FATHER, FILL MY HEART WITH COMPASSION AND LOVE AS YOU USE ME TO HELP COMFORT THE BROKEN, THE HURTING, AND THE WEARY.

NOVEMBER 6

A good person produces good things
from the treasury of a good heart.
LUKE 6:45 NLT

Our hearts are good because our amazingly good God abides there, enabling us to lead a life of love. The best way to cultivate love in this big and lonely world is to sow seeds of love everywhere we go! Our sovereign God puts us where He wants us: in the right place at the right time to love the people who are right in front of us. He directs our steps according to His purpose, which is to bring the *greatest* harvest of love.

FATHER, THANK YOU FOR LOVING ME
AND PREPARING MY HEART
TO PRODUCE GOOD THINGS,
TO REFLECT YOUR KINDNESS AND
YOUR LOVE TO OTHERS.

NOVEMBER 7

The love of the LORD remains forever
with those who fear Him.
PSALM 103:17 NLT

The Love that *changed the course of history* and, today, *changes the world* heart by heart is the love that, by God's Spirit, lives within us. Wherever we are, people around us need God's love right now. Every person without Him has a heart that feels empty. Every person seeking Him has a heart ready to see Him. And every person who knows Him wants to know Him better. God knows each person's need. We just have to follow His lead!

FATHER, YOUR LOVE IS FAITHFUL AND FOREVER. GIVE ME GUIDANCE AND GRACE TO BE A TOUCH OF THAT LOVE TO EVERY PERSON IN MY LIFE.

NOVEMBER 8

You are a God of forgiveness...
full of love and mercy.
NEHEMIAH 9:17

Forgiveness, love, and mercy. *Day after brand-new day.* God doesn't cease being kind to us on days when we're tired and don't even have the strength to sign in for the love walk we're called to finish. Often, life's demands truly *are* too great for us... *because our good and gracious Father wants us to learn to depend on Him*. He has the goods that give us the strength to *do* good...and He faithfully refills our hearts with His love as needed!

FATHER, I CAN'T MAKE IT THROUGH MY DAYS WITHOUT YOU! GIVE ME THE STRENGTH TO DO YOUR WILL BY THE POWER OF YOUR LOVE.

NOVEMBER 9

Tell the world about His wondrous love!
ISAIAH 12:4

If we are Christ-followers, that's our mandate from heaven: tell the world about God's amazing love! Nothing more wonderful than God's love exists. Nothing matters more than telling the world about His love. And nothing we can work for, win, or want is *more valuable*. God's love is all we need—and it's what we are to praise and proclaim. Finally, God's love is all we need to make this world a brighter, more beautiful place.

FATHER, GIVE ME WAYS TO SHOWER YOUR LOVE ON THE LIVES AROUND ME EVERY DAY.

NOVEMBER 10

*We can't round up enough containers
to hold everything God generously pours
into our lives through the Holy Spirit!*
ROMANS 5:5 THE MESSAGE

Our God is beyond generous! We have, for instance, all the love we need to live confident lives that honor Him—with plenty of love left over to share. *And that's why we're here*: to give, give, *give* in order to point people to our *generously giving God*. He doesn't hold back His love from us because He wants us to hand it out! So do the simple kindness. Look around and be the one who steps up to help. Listen to your heart and follow the prompting of the Holy Spirit. You can pour out God's love pretty much *everywhere*.

FATHER, KEEP MY EYES OPEN AND MY
SPIRIT SENSITIVE TO OPPORTUNITIES
TO SHARE YOUR LOVE WITH PEOPLE
WHO NEED IT MOST.

NOVEMBER 11

O Lord, we love to do Your will!
Our hearts' desire is to glorify Your name.
ISAIAH 26:8

When our deepest desire is to glorify God, we need to remember that our love for Him and for others will be the evidence. In fact, God's will is summed up in His greatest commands: love God and love others. We can mess up a lot of things, make a lot of mistakes, miss the mark a lot of times... but if we keep getting up to keep giving love, our lives will bring glory to *Him*.

FATHER, I WANT YOUR LOVE TO GUIDE
MY HEART SO THAT MY LIFE WILL
BRING YOU GLORY!

NOVEMBER 12

If you brag, brag of this only:
That you understand and know Me.
I'm GOD, and I act in loyal love.
JEREMIAH 9:24 THE MESSAGE

Everything we go through in this journey of life gives us a better understanding of God and—without fail—a far clearer picture of His love. When we see Him deliver and redeem, provide and protect, and when we experience His comfort and hope, we realize more completely that *God loves us with all His heart*. When a storm rages around us, there's a revelation when we look above it: God is saying, "You need me most...*and I need you to know that*."

FATHER, TEACH MY HEART TO
UNDERSTAND MORE COMPLETELY THE
FULLNESS AND FAITHFULNESS OF
YOUR LOVE, SO I CAN MORE TRULY
REFLECT IT TO OTHERS.

NOVEMBER 13

*Let everything you say be good and helpful,
so that your words will be an encouragement.*
EPHESIANS 4:29 NLT

Encouraging words—when we say them, when we hear them, and even when we think them—are splashes of love in our day. Good words can be truly life-giving, and speaking them is one of the most refreshing ways we can show God's love to others. Let's start our day with prayerful thoughts that become perfect words that share the power of God's love to *everyone* in our lives!

FATHER, HELP ME ENCOURAGE OTHERS
WITH WORDS THAT ARE LIFE-GIVING
AND LOVE-BRINGING!

NOVEMBER 14

*May our Lord Jesus Christ Himself
and God our Father...
help you in every good thing
you say and do.*
II THESSALONIANS 2:16-17

God doesn't ask us to give something to other people that He doesn't give to us in downpours! In fact, we whom God has adopted as His children will never suffer droughts of *any* good thing. He's here to help us every day—to help us do good things, to love in good ways, and to share His grace and kindness with *everything* we say.

FATHER, YOUR LOVE IS THE GOOD
IN ALL I SAY AND DO, MERELY HINTING
THE INFINITE GOOD IN YOU.
I LOVE YOU, LORD!

NOVEMBER 15

The homes of the upright—how blessed!
Their houses brim with wealth
and a generosity that never runs dry.
PSALM 112:2-3 THE MESSAGE

Generosity and love bring blessings that never run dry. We don't need a put-together life, a perfect home, or a prominent position to be generous with God's love. *We simply have to be willing to let Him work through us.* God's love welcomes everyone at all times: do we? His love makes room for the needy at any cost: do we? And loving people with His love is our highest purpose: do our lives reflect that?

FATHER, GIVE ME A HEART THAT'S
HUMBLE AND READY TO SERVE
WHENEVER I SEE A CHANCE
TO SHARE YOUR LOVE.

NOVEMBER 16

*It is a fine thing when people are nice
to you with good motives
and sincere hearts.*
GALATIANS 4:18

We love because *God loves us*. We do good because *God is good*. The love we share with our words and actions is authentic because it's *all for God* and because *glorifying Him is our motive*. His light shines in our acts of love and compassion, and the world sees it. When our lives point the way to God through the power of love, we can know absolute joy. May the desire to obey God and the joy that results inspire our actions every day!

FATHER, MAKE MY LIFE A BEACON
OF YOUR LOVE AND GOODNESS,
PROMPTING PRAISE TO YOU!

NOVEMBER 17

*Remind each other of God's goodness,
and be thankful.*
EPHESIANS 5:4

We can remind each other how good God is and how much He loves us with very simple actions. A phone call, a brief text, an invitation to lunch, or a quick note can be a lifeline of hope, a light in a person's darkness, and a reminder that God hasn't forgotten them. We who have named Jesus our Savior can never be separated from His love, but it can sure feel like we are when life gets tough. So when we feel strong, let's help someone else along, for God didn't design us to journey alone.

FATHER, GIVE ME STRENGTH TO HELP OTHERS STAND BY SHOWING THEM THE FAITHFULNESS OF YOUR LOVE.

NOVEMBER 18

Give, and you will receive.
LUKE 6:38 NLT

God will always outlove us! We can never love Him more than He loves us. That's why we can count on Him to fill us to overflowing with His love. That's why we can let our lives become a vessel for Him to pour His love through to others! When we love, we receive more love, and the world around us gets more beautiful—and that's a nice return on our investment.

FATHER, GIVE ME A HEART THAT FREELY
AND GENEROUSLY GIVES OUT
YOUR LOVE. I ASK YOU TO KEEP
POURING YOUR LOVE THROUGH ME
INTO THE LIVES OF OTHERS.

NOVEMBER 19

I will bless the Lord who guides me.
PSALM 16:7 NLT

We know God is guiding us by the love markers we notice along the way—if we look for them. Every tough experience we walk through brings us closer to Him—if we let it. Every lonely season brings us to a better understanding of His love—if we are open. And the more we understand God's infinite, incredible love, the more faithful we'll be to share it—and our lives will become ever brighter as the beauty of God's love shines through them!

FATHER, THANK YOU FOR FAITHFULLY GUIDING ME ON A PATH FRAGRANT WITH YOUR AMAZING LOVE. HELP ME ALWAYS SHARE IT ALONG THE WAY— AND HELP ME ALWAYS LEARN FROM ALL I EXPERIENCE ON THAT PATH.

NOVEMBER 20

*You enlarged my path under me,
so my feet did not slip.*
PSALM 18:36 NKJV

Maybe God makes the path beneath our feet wide so there's room for us to walk side-by-side with someone through life. Maybe we simply need each other every day to lock arms in faith, to hold each other's hand, to give a hug when we need one. Maybe—just maybe—the love we give others helps keep us from falling.

FATHER, THANK YOU FOR GIVING US YOUR LIFE-SAVING, HEART-HEALING, FAITH-BUILDING LOVE. KEEP ME MINDFUL AND READY TO GENEROUSLY GIVE YOUR LOVE TO OTHERS

NOVEMBER 21

God sees into my heart right now.
I CORINTHIANS 13:12

God sees all that our hearts have to give—and He gives, *in overwhelming measure*, all that our hearts need from Him. He is our Savior and our Strength who enables us to see people the way He does. He can, for instance, reveal to us the love that people need and then move our hearts to kindness and good deeds. Knowing that—sometimes using us—He'll always meet the need, we can peacefully follow wherever He leads.

FATHER, YOU SEE THE NEEDS OF EVERY
PERSON'S HEART. PREPARE ME AND
POINT ME TO THOSE PEOPLE
YOU WOULD HAVE ME LOVE TODAY
WITH YOUR LOVE AND GRACE.

NOVEMBER 22

Give yourselves to the gifts God gives you.
I CORINTHIANS 14:1 THE MESSAGE

You have God-given gifts to give the world! God *designed all of them with love* for the purpose of drawing people to *His perfect, powerful, life-giving love.* The special qualities in you make your life shine with the light of His presence. So go wherever God's Spirit leads, love the people He brings into your life...and let Him build up His kingdom through you!

FATHER, ALL THE GIFTS YOU'VE GIVEN ME CAN EXHIBIT THE POWER OF YOUR LOVE. PLEASE HELP ME USE THEM FREELY AND FAITHFULLY WHEN AND WHERE YOU WANT ME TO.

NOVEMBER 23

How joyful are those who fear the Lord....
They share freely and give generously
to those in need.
PSALM 112:1,9 NLT

When we love God with all we are—recognizing how much He loves us—we find the *greatest* inspiration for loving others. So let's give love *exuberantly* and in *extravagant* portions. Let's overflow the banks of someone's despair with kindness and compassion. Let's encourage our discouraged neighbors and light up our shadowy neighborhoods. Let us be the God-fearing, and faithful world-changers God has called us to be, exercising fully the power of His love within us.

> FATHER, PURE JOY COMES WHEN I
> SHARE YOUR PERFECT LOVE.
> THANK YOU THAT THAT'S THE WAY
> LOVE WORKS—AND MAY THAT
> LOVE-RELATED JOY ME EVERY DAY
> TO LOVE GENEROUSLY.

NOVEMBER 24

Give us help for the hard task...
In God we'll do our very best.
PSALM 108:12-13 THE MESSAGE

It won't always be easy to show people love and shower kindness. We're not wired to get along with everybody, but we are *required* to love them—to want the best for them, to want salvation for them, and to want them to know peace and joy. Loving others is God's commandment to us, and He gives us the grace to fulfill it. After all, He doesn't call us to love only the people who are easy to love. We don't get excused from loving others just because they're harder to love. Those people simply give us a greater reason to *fully depend on God* as we share His love.

FATHER, HELP ME STAY HUMBLE,
FAITHFUL, AND GRACIOUS AS—
IN OBEDIENCE—I LOVE OTHERS IN
YOUR STRENGTH, NOT MY OWN.

NOVEMBER 25

My God is changeless in His love for me.
PSALM 59:10

Change is constant in our lives and circumstances—and at times we are left completely unsure about where God is taking us. But no matter how darkened the road stretching out in front of us remains, we can know the light of God's love *right where we are*. We can also choose to appreciate life's changes and unknowns as lessons in how to be sure and secure in His *changeless* love. And that unchanging love will mean blessings ahead.

FATHER, I TRUST YOU WITH ALL MY HEART, AND I AM BLESSED TO HAVE THE PEACE THAT COMES WITH KNOWING THE FAITHFULNESS OF YOUR LOVE.

NOVEMBER 26

We meditate upon Your kindness
and Your love.
PSALM 48:9

Think about the kind and loving things God has done for you—the little things you didn't expect, the big things that made you cry with joy, the sweet things that made you smile. *He loves you*, and He loves to show you His love in lots of ways every day. There isn't a moment in time when He doesn't have time for you... or when He won't take the time to send you a love note.

FATHER, IS THE WAYS YOU SHOW ME YOUR LOVE SHOW ME HOW ATTENTIVE AND THOUGHTFUL YOU ARE. THANK YOU FOR LOVING ME—AND THANK YOU FOR ALL THE WAYS YOU SEND ME GLIMPSES OF YOUR LOVE THROUGHOUT THE DAY.

NOVEMBER 27

GOD is the real thing—
the living God, the eternal King.
JEREMIAH 10:10 THE MESSAGE

Genuine. Authentic. *Real.* It's hard to find anything that meets those criteria today. Anything except *God's love.* We can *say* that love exists without Him, but that kind of love is not the *best.* Apart from Him we can't share love that is truly good, life-giving, and eternal. Only His Spirit within us produces that kind of pure, imperishable fruit that is evidence of God's grace in our lives.

FATHER, I NEED YOU IF I AM TO SHARE YOUR GENUINE, AUTHENTIC, REAL, LIFE-CHANGING LOVE. THANK YOU THAT I CAN DRAW CLOSE TO YOU AND STAY CONNECTED WITH YOU SO THE WORLD CAN SEE YOUR LIFE IN ME.

NOVEMBER 28

The LORD leads with unfailing love
and faithfulness.
PSALM 25:10 NLT

God's love is the perfect leader. By the power of His Spirit, our loving God opens our eyes to the needs of others, gives us courage to follow through to meet those needs, and guides us to the most effective way to tell people about God. *His love never fails.* He will lead us along a path to His *best* for us—to full-scale contentment, fulfillment of purpose, and *fullness of joy!*

FATHER, THANK YOU THAT
YOU LEAD ME WITH LOVE AND
FAITHFULNESS. THANK YOU THAT
YOU LEAD ME TO YOUR BEST.
MY HEART REJOICES IN YOU.

NOVEMBER 29

*Learn to do good, to be fair, and to help
the poor, the fatherless, and widows.*
ISAIAH 1:17

Love looks down in order to lift others *up*.
After all, no one person is more precious
to God than any other. Through His eyes
of love, we look the same, and He calls us
to do the same while we walk this earth.
We are here to help the poor, the fatherless, and widows. We are hear to do good,
and one of the best acts we can do is help
each other see the faithfulness of *God's
love*. His unfailing and unconditional love
brings hope, comfort, warmth, and peace
to the hearts of the hurting and to the brokenness of the burdened. Let's live to *lift*,
light, and *love one another*!

FATHER, TEACH ME YOUR WAY OF LOVE,
GIVE ME YOUR EYES TO SEE,
AND BLESS ME TO DO THE WORK OF
YOUR HANDS.

NOVEMBER 30

*The ways of right-living people glow with light;
the longer they live, the brighter they shine.*
PROVERBS 4:18 THE MESSAGE

It's fun to think that every little thing we do with God's love glows with God's light. We can put the light of God's presence in a smile, an act of kindness, a hug, a long talk, or a short visit. Spreading the brightness of joy like that changes the landscape of our day. May our light burn brightly, testifying to the truth that God is *magnanimously* good—and our lives can be *manifestations* of His love.

FATHER, LET MY LIFE BE BRIGHTER
EVERY DAY WITH THE LIGHT OF YOUR
WONDERFUL LOVE.

DECEMBER 1

Love will last forever!
I CORINTHIANS 13:8 NLT

God made His eternal love most obvious in the gift of His Son for our salvation. A dim shadow of that gift are those we give at Christmastime. The love gifts symbolize lasts longer than the joy and excitement of giving gifts. It lasts longer than the laughter, the memories, and the long evenings in front of the fire. The love of God that we share with others keeps on making a difference after the lights are taken down and the chill is no longer in the air. *Love comes from God.* And when hearts are changed by the power of His love, heavenly rejoicing goes on forever!

FATHER, PLEASE HELP ME LIVE WITH YOUR LOVE AS THE FOCUS OF EVERYTHING I DO, SO THAT ALL I DO MAKES AN ETERNAL DIFFERENCE.

DECEMBER 2

*Keep right on loving others
as long as life lasts,
so that you will get your full reward.*
HEBREWS 6:11

Earthly gain is a fleeting, fading reward.
We can work long and hard for the things
we dream of having, but unless we spend
our time loving *people*, our hearts won't
enjoy the greatest rewards of all. A life of
love—a life invested in people—lights the
way to God. Nothing else we do—no other
investment—can bring a more *beautiful*
reward than knowing we did what our Father
wanted us to do.

FATHER, GIVE ME A HEART TO LOVE
LIKE YOU LOVE SO THAT MY LIFE
BRINGS YOU HONOR AND PRAISE.

DECEMBER 3

Pay all your debts except the debt of love to others—never finish paying that!

ROMANS 13:8

Love makes more deposits of good into this world than *any* other thing we do! Love that reflects God's love is kind, compassionate, generous, hopeful, good, and forgiving, and blessed are those in whom we invest this kind of love. The return for these investments is the joy of knowing God is *pleased* with our obedience and *praised* for the love we share. After all, by God's grace, the investing of *His love will lead to Him*. His love created us, saved us, and changed us, and now God uses human and imperfect reflections of His love to nevertheless change lives *through* us.

FATHER, I WANT YOUR LOVE TO FLOW THROUGH MY LIFE CONTINUOUSLY AND ABUNDANTLY! PLEASE USE ME TO HELP OTHERS RECOGNIZE AND RUN TO YOUR GREAT LOVE.

DECEMBER 4

Let the loveliness of our Lord, our God,
rest on us.
PSALM 90:17 THE MESSAGE

The world can see the light and loveliness of God in you. More specifically, they see calmness in your countenance, brightness in your smile, and the warmth of your heart. Further evidence of His presence in you is the *love you give*. Loving with God's unconditional and persistent love touches hearts and opens people to knowing more about Him, the One who has the power to save a soul and the grace to sustain it.

FATHER, PLEASE HAVE THE LOVELINESS
OF JESUS REST ON ME.
PLEASE FILL MY LIFE WITH THE LIGHT
OF YOUR LOVE SO THAT HEARTS ARE
DRAWN TO YOU.

DECEMBER 5

*Dress yourselves in Christ,
and be up and about!*
ROMANS 13:14 THE MESSAGE

The love of our Savior is the most beautiful thing we can fill our lives with and wrap ourselves in! So every morning may we be mindful of wrapping ourselves in God's love, of dressing ourselves in Christ. The world needs to see God's love in action, so may we be the ones offering a helping hand, giving our time, showing kindness, and opening our homes. Everything we do communicates messages. May ours always be written with love!

FATHER, SHOW ME EVERY OPPORTUNITY TO HELP SOMEONE IN NEED, SOMEONE WHOSE HEART NEEDS TO BY TOUCHED BY YOUR LOVE.

DECEMBER 6

*Through Christ, all the kindness of God
has been poured out upon us.*
ROMANS 1:5

Christ is God's kindness revealed. The Almighty's indescribable, eternal love became less distant and far more personal through His ultimate act of kindness... poured out on us through Jesus' death on the cross for our salvation. We, too, are to act with kindness—and we can never truly know the impact of our *being kind to others*. God uses small acts of kindness to make big changes in hearts.

So let's keep being *kind*—trusting God to use our acts of kindness to prepare those we are *kind* to—to receive the *greatest love ever known*.

FATHER, LET MY ACTIONS, MY WORDS,
AND MY LIFE BE REFLECTIONS
OF YOUR LOVE AND KINDNESS FOR
YOUR KINGDOM'S GROWTH AND
YOUR GREAT GLORY.

DECEMBER 7

By this My Father is glorified,
that you bear much fruit.
JOHN 15:8 NKJV

Followers of Jesus are called—among
other things—to *love* people and to *trust*
God. We don't get to decide who and
who doesn't populate our life lives, but
we get the distinct and divine privilege
of loving every single one of them. God
will use some of these people to teach us
patience, while others will help us grow in
grace. Life is about learning to love better—and may some of the fruit be nourished lives and saved souls.

FATHER, HELP ME SURRENDER EVERY
DAY TO YOU, TRUSTING THAT—
UNDER YOUR CARE—MY LIFE WILL
BEAR MUCH FRUIT.

DECEMBER 8

*"With everlasting love
I will have compassion on you,"
says the Lord, your Redeemer.*
ISAIAH 54:8 NLT

God's love spills over with compassion for us who desperately need and want to be loved. God's love is, for instance, filled to the top and overflowing in forgiveness. His love is immeasurably more than we deserve—and He loves us no matter *how many times* we fail. Nothing we do can empty His heart of the love He has for us because *everlasting* means His love is on automatic refill. So rest in His love today and love Him in return by not only loving Him but also by *loving others*.

FATHER, YOUR LOVE IS AMAZING AND TRUE. MAY I LIVE—MAY I SPEAK AND ACT—WITH COMPASSION SO OTHERS CAN SEE YOUR LOVE IN ME.

DECEMBER 9

*Your steadfast love, O Lord,
is as great as all the heavens.*

PSALM 36:5

All the heavens can't contain it, the seas can't hold it, and the skies are no measure for it: God's love truly is infinite and infinitely beyond our comprehension. It can't be depleted, detached from our lives, or destroyed by any spiritual force. Your love is ours for eternity, yet it enters the world at large through *our lives*. Let's open the floodgates of love today by what we do, how we live, and the words we choose!

FATHER, YOUR LOVE IS IMMEASURABLE
AND STEADFAST. I WANT IT BE
THE ONE THING THAT INFLUENCES
EVERYTHING IN MY LIFE.

DECEMBER 10

Be strong and steady,
always abounding in the Lord's work.
I CORINTHIANS 15:58

We Jesus followers aren't superheroes, but we have a power far beyond and of theirs—and our power is *real*. And our power is God's love that can move hearts to eternal life, remove mountains of guilt through grace, and move heaven and earth to rescue a single lost soul. God gives His love to us *freely* and tells us to give it to others *fully*, without reservation or judgment. That's our lifelong mission: *love one another*.

FATHER, YOUR WORK FOR ME IS TO
YIELD TO YOU SO THAT YOU CAN
POUR YOUR LOVE THROUGH US AND
INTO THE LIVES OF OTHERS. LET ME
BE DILIGENT ABOUT BOTH LIVING
WITH YOU AS LORD AND LOVING
UNCONDITIONALLY.

DECEMBER 11

When God our Savior revealed His kindness and love, He saved us, not because of the righteous things we had done, but because of His mercy.

TITUS 3:4-5 NLT

By grace alone—that's how we are able to love the world *God's* way. His love is kind, merciful, unconditional, and joyful. We don't have to earn it, nor should *anyone* feel they have to. God's love isn't given according to some kind of reward system; it's readily available to all to restore and redeem at all times. Let's be kind... *just because*. Let's love others... *without expectations*. Let's glorify God... in *everything* we do.

FATHER, I AM GRATEFUL YOU DON'T LOVE ME BASED ON ANYTHING I HAVE DONE, BUT SIMPLY BECAUSE OF YOUR MERCY. PLEASE HELP ME TO EXTEND GRACE TO PEOPLE AND TO LOVE THEM THE WAY YOU LOVE ME—WITH COMPASSION AND KINDNESS.

DECEMBER 12

*Christ became a human being
and lived here on earth among us and
was full of loving forgiveness and truth.*

JOHN 1:14

If our lives are going to be filled with what's good and true, love is what we need to choose! Love forgives and moves forward. Love listens and speaks wisdom. Love cares and carries burdens. Love takes time to seek , and love does the right thing whatever the cost. When we draw close to God, *love* is drawn out of us, love that enables us to meet the needs of others.

FATHER, HELP ME TO LIVE MY LIFE
WITH YOUR LOVE AND YOUR TRUTH
SHAPING MY HEART, DIRECTING MY
ACTIONS, AND GUIDING MY WORDS.

DECEMBER 13

*Generous people plan
to do what is generous.*
ISAIAH 32:8 NLT

We can decide to do good things that just might inspire even more good in the world. We can plan to be generous with our time, our resources, and our talents. We can be determined to be patient, kind, and forgiving. But we can't do any of this alone—and thankfully, we don't have to. God is our steady and sure Source of strength—and our sound Foundation for a life that shines with love!

FATHER, GIVE ME A HEART LIKE YOURS.
HELP ME BE GENEROUS AS I HELP
OTHERS AND AS I DO THE GOOD YOU
CALL ME TO DO WITH THE GIFTS
YOU'VE GIVEN ME.

DECEMBER 14

Let your light shine for all to see.
For the glory of the Lord rises to shine on you.
ISAIAH 60:1 NLT

Let your light shine! It's God who will get the praise when we love others and do the right thing. Fill the world with the brightness of His presence! It's mercy that will set hearts on a path to seek Him. Let your face beam with joy and your days glow with kindness—it's the way God will change us, and bless us, with *good*.

FATHER, MAKE MY LIFE RESPLENDENT WITH THE LIGHT OF YOUR LOVE AND GOODNESS SO THAT SEARCHING SOULS FIND THEIR WAY TO YOU.

DECEMBER 15

*Do good, and lend, hoping for nothing in return;
and your reward will be great.*
LUKE 6:35 NKJV

Needs are all around us, and the miracle of God's love is in our hearts. May we use the latter to address the former! We can't let ourselves get so busy that we forget or ignore the power we have—by God's grace—to make a difference. Is there a nice thing you've thought about doing for a friend or neighbor, but haven't gotten around to? Let's drop something from the to-do list by dropping some love into that person's day!

> FATHER, PLEASE USE ME TO BLESS PEOPLE WITH YOUR SWEET LOVE. HELP ME BE SENSITIVE TO YOUR SPIRIT'S LEADING, HIS GENTLE NUDGES, AND THE COMMANDS TO LOVE THAT ARE IN YOUR WORD— AND FOLLOW THROUGH WITH JOY!

DECEMBER 16

No matter what I say, what I believe,
and what I do, I'm bankrupt without love.
I CORINTHIANS 13:3 THE MESSAGE

Love matters more than anything else we can be involved in, and love gives more than anything the world offers. God's love gives every person a sense of purpose and a feeling of value. This love gives light, hope, and joy! It gives the darkness no place to go, dispelling it with one act of kindness, one encouraging word, and one generous deed at a time. A little bit, several times each day... *let's give love away!*

FATHER, LOVE IS THE WAY YOU CAN USE ME TO SHOW OTHERS THE WAY TO YOUR HEART. LET ME BE FAITHFUL IN LOVING YOU AND LOVING PEOPLE EVERY DAY.

DECEMBER 18

*Be full of love for others, following the example
of Christ who loved you and gave Himself
to God as a sacrifice to take away your sins.*

EPHESIANS 5:2

Let our hearts be full, our feet be willing, and our hands be faithful as we live a life of love as God commands. *Love is what we're here to do.* We don't have time to hesitate, and we can't let ourselves hurry us past the chances we have to love people. Love has a way of slowing moments down, though, because love moves from heart to heart. And *things in the heart last*.

FATHER, YOUR LOVE IS EVERLASTING
AND ALWAYS KIND. HELP ME NOT MISS
THE CHANCES YOU GIVE ME TO SHARE
IT WITH EVERYONE IN MY LIFE.

DECEMBER 17

Light shines in the darkness for the godly.
They are generous, compassionate,
and righteous.
PSALM 112:4 NLT

It is a privilege to be loved by Jesus and to love like He does. To be chosen and called to bring His beautiful love to this world is a privilege we can act on with absolute, unshakeable joy. And we experience such joy as a sweet byproduct of His love and the unwavering assurance of His presence with us. He's the celebration of our hearts, and we have *every reason* to rejoice in the love He has given us—and now we *live* to *give*!

FATHER, THE LOVE OF JESUS IS THE JOY OF MY HEART AND THE PASSION FUELING MY PURPOSE. LET ME SHARE HIS LOVE GENEROUSLY EVERY DAY.

DECEMBER 19

I've loved you the way My Father has loved Me.
Make yourselves at home in My love.

JOHN 15:9 THE MESSAGE

The love for us that Jesus demonstrated on the cross is our redemption and our refuge. He also considers it our *home*. And at home in Jesus' love, we can drop every façade and lay bare every weakness. We might feel a little uncomfortable, but we can rest assured that no matter *what we do or don't do*, Jesus will *never* ask us to leave. In fact, God's love is the place we go to be safe, held, and forgiven. It's the love of a perfect Father, and it's our haven in an imperfect world.

FATHER, THANK YOU FOR YOUR LOVE
AND GRACE—AND FOR YOUR SON
WHOSE DEATH ON THE CROSS IS
A VIVID PICTURE OF THAT LOVE AND
GRACE. I AM BLESSED TO KNOW YOUR
LOVE—AND THERE'S NO OTHER PLACE
I WOULD RATHER BE.

DECEMBER 20

Be still, and know that I am God.
PSALM 46:10 NKJV

The blessing of stillness and calm comes with knowing that God loves us. His love floods our souls with peace as we consider His promise of eternal life and remind ourselves of His presence with us always. God's love keeps us centered on our true purpose on this earth, which is to *love others* with this heavenly love that brings light, joy, hope, and every good thing every heart *truly* needs. God's love is the perfect gift—and it's ours to give!

FATHER, AS I PRAISE YOU AND REST IN YOUR PERFECT LOVE, PLEASE HELP ME SHARE YOUR LOVE WITH OTHERS JOYFULLY AND FAITHFULLY.

DECEMBER 21

*Abiding love surrounds those
who trust in the Lord.*
PSALM 32:10

Abiding love—what a lovely phrase! God's love will stay; it will neither fade away nor depart from us. His love surrounds who trust Him and know His powerful presence with them. Let's surround the people we love with *that kind of love* that offers security, that makes them feel safe and *important*. God puts us together in a family, He brings us together as friends, and He pulls us together through pain, circumstances, and prayer. *We're not alone*—and God's love makes sure we don't feel like we are.

FATHER, TEACH ME TO KEEP MY HEART,
MY HOME, AND MY ARMS OPEN WIDE
WITH YOUR LOVE.

DECEMBER 22

Everything we know about God's Word is
summed up in a single sentence:
Love others as you love yourself.
GALATIANS 5:14 THE MESSAGE

Be God's love today! Don't overthink the
how or the where. Instead, rest in the fact
that He's guiding every step you take. Your
prayerful heart will point you in the right
direction, and He'll be faithful to show you
the need He wants You to address. That
need may be at home or at work, while
you're running errands or walking through
the neighborhood. God sees every heart
everywhere, and He knows who needs His
love delivered through you.

FATHER, KEEP MY HEART HUMBLE,
MY SPIRIT FAITHFUL, AND MY HANDS
WILLING TO SHARE YOUR LOVE
WHEREVER AND HOWEVER YOU LEAD.

DECEMBER 23

I am the light of the world.
If you follow Me, you won't have to walk
in darkness, because you will have the light
that leads to life.

JOHN 8:12 NLT

People who know Jesus as Savior and Lord—and who have His Spirit living within—shine from the inside out. The love that saved the world lives *within* you, and it can be the bright spot in someone's day, a beacon of hope in someone's discouragement, or the floodlight that washes over a lost soul, leading them to the *life* they see in you. We never know how God will use our lives to help others, but we know to always offer that help with kindness and love.

FATHER, FILL ME WITH YOUR LIGHT
AND YOUR LOVE TODAY. PLEASE USE
MY LIFE TO BRING OTHERS TO YOU.

DECEMBER 24

Let love be your highest goal!
I CORINTHIANS 14:1 NLT

Life is all about learning to love; our purpose on this planet is to love others; and every command God gives revolves around *one* thing: LOVE! He has made it very clear: love is a *big deal*. He put it this way: "Let love by your highest goal." Having read that, how can we wonder what to do with our lives? We are to love. Nothing is more important than love, no goal is higher than love, and there's *no greater way* to love our *great God* than to obey Him by *loving others*.

FATHER, YOUR LOVE IS THE BEST PART OF LIFE AND THE HIGHEST PURPOSE YOU CAN GIVE ME FOR THIS LIFE. LET YOUR LOVE FLOW THROUGH ME FOR THE GOOD OF THE PEOPLE I COME IN CONTACT WITH AND FOR YOUR GREAT GLORY.

DECEMBER 25

This is how God loved the world:
He gave His one and only Son,
so that everyone who believes in Him
will not perish but have eternal life.

JOHN 3:16 NLT

God's love is greater than any love we can describe or even imagine. God showed us this indescribably and unmeasurable love by giving what none of us could comprehend giving: His Son. His ultimate act of love was more beautiful than any act of love we've ever witnessed: death on a cross. And this act of love reveals a degree of kindness greater than any of us could have hoped to receive: the grace and mercy of forgiveness. When we receive His love, when we acknowledge our sin and Jesus' complete and perfect sacrifice for our sins, and when we invite Him into our hearts, we receive the astounding gift of eternal life. We. Are. *Blessed.*

FATHER, I PRAISE YOU FOR THE GIFT OF YOUR LOVE IN THE LIFE AND THE DEATH AND THE RESURRECTION LIFE OF YOUR SON. ALL GLORY TO YOU, FOREVER AND EVER.

DECEMBER 26

*The Lord sees every heart and
understands and knows every thought.*

I CHRONICLES 28:9

God's love shows us how to *truly* love others. Oh, we can't see what their hearts are
crying out for, but as we stay close to the
One who *can*, we are to simply be faithful
to do what He leads us to do. God loves
the people we love even more than we do,
and we can trust Him to guide us in how to
love them *best*.

FATHER, WITH EACH PERSON YOU
PUT IN MY PATH, PLEASE SHOW ME
HOW TO LOVE THAT PERSON IN
THOSE PARTICULAR CIRCUMSTANCES
IN THE BEST POSSIBLE WAY. LET MY
SPIRIT LISTEN CLOSELY TO YOU, HEAR
CLEARLY, AND ACT FAITHFULLY.

DECEMBER 27

God has not given us a spirit of fear,
but of power and of love and of a sound mind.
II TIMOTHY 1:7 NKJV

Our heavenly Father knows we get weary. He also knows when we need to be held and loved by Him until we're back to the point where we have the strength to love others. In our down times, we can look up and know He is *everything* we need. We can also know that He doesn't want us to be afraid (a side effect of weariness!), but that He wants us to know His power and love. So if you're weary right now, get settled in the lap of His love. Sit there quietly until your spirit gathers courage enough that you can go on—*fearlessly!*

FATHER, WRAP ME IN YOUR LOVE
UNTIL I KNOW YOUR STRENGTH IN MY
HEART. I TRUST YOU TO BE ALL I NEED,
WHATEVER I FACE.

DECEMBER 28

Now abide faith, hope, love, these three;
but the greatest of these is love.
I CORINTHIANS 13:13 NKJV

Love God and people with a *joyful* spirit. Live God and people with a *thankful* heart. Pray with a *fervent* faith. And know that—by God's grace—all that you do to share His love is all you really *need* to do. God will always step in to help. So every time you take a deep breath, look into a person's eyes, and listen... Or every time you stop what you're doing to write the simple words *I love you* on a piece of paper... And every time you interrupt your day to love someone with God's love... *heaven rejoices*.

FATHER, YOUR LOVE IS A GIFT LIKE NO OTHER. BECAUSE YOU LOVE ME, I CAN KNOW PEACE, GUIDANCE, HOPE, HEALING, FORGIVENESS, GRACE, AND SO MUCH MORE.. I WANT TO GIVE YOUR LOVE TO THOSE PEOPLE YOU GIVE TO ME...SO THEIR HEARTS CAN RECEIVE YOUR LIFE-GIVING AND ETERNAL-LIFE-GIVING GIFT.

DECEMBER 29

Whatever is good and perfect
comes to us from God.
JAMES 1:17

God's love—a gift to us from God Himself—is good and perfect. It is also always the best way to respond to people and the kindest way to live. We have many chances every day to do simple, loving acts. Oh, we might stumble over a wild emotion or two, but as quickly as we ask God to forgive us, we are forgiven—and in the next moment comes another opportunity to love. Never give up even when you find yourself loving with less than God's perfect love. Never give up because God's love will never fail you.

FATHER, MAKE MY LIFE A REFLECTION
OF YOUR GOOD AND PERFECT LOVE.

DECEMBER 30

Live generously.
LUKE 6:30 THE MESSAGE

Open your heart and love with every bit of it. Don't be afraid to give even when you know you won't get anything in return. Be courageously kind. Be brave about loving others because extending love is never wrong. God is love, and there is no real love without Him. The ultimate gift of God's love, Jesus calls us to "live generously" as He did, giving His life to ransom us from sin and death. May we follow His example and obey His command. May we live—and love—generously.

FATHER, LET ME LIVE TO GIVE LOVE GENEROUSLY. AND AS I LIVE EACH DAY, MAY PEOPLE LOOK AT ME AND EASILY SEE THAT YOU ARE THE JOY OF MY HEART AND MY GREATEST REWARD.

DECEMBER 31

Don't hide your light! Let it shine for all;
let your good deeds glow for all to see,
so that they will praise your heavenly Father.
MATTHEW 5:15-16

We must see to it that the people we know, *know they are loved* by the God who created them, who wants to be in relationship with them, who sent His Son to die for them, and who desires to spend eternity with them Love—God's love—can do more to light the darkness than *any other power* on earth. May we who know the power of God's love make everything we do about love! May we let it filter our words and be the focus of our actions. May God's love guide how we treat people and be the reason why our lives glow with joy!

> FATHER, I LOVE YOU. I COMMIT MY LIFE TO YOU AGAIN TODAY. HELP ME LIVE OUT MY DEEPEST DESIRE: I WANT TO LIVE THANKFULLY, JOYFULLY, AND LOVINGLY... FOR YOUR GREAT GLORY.

LIVE YOUR FAITH

Dear Friend,

This book was prayerfully crafted with you, the reader, in mind—every word, every sentence, every page—was thoughtfully written, designed, and packaged to encourage you...right where you are this very moment. At DaySpring, our vision is to see every person experience the life-changing message of God's love. So, as we worked through rough drafts, design changes, edits, and details, we prayed for you to deeply experience His unfailing love, indescribable peace, and pure joy. It is our sincere hope that through these Truth-filled pages your heart will be blessed, knowing that God cares about you—your desires and disappointments, your challenges and dreams.

He knows. He cares. He loves you unconditionally.

BLESSINGS!
THE DAYSPRING BOOK TEAM

Additional copies of this book and
other DaySpring titles can be purchased
at fine bookstores everywhere.
Order online at dayspring.com
or
by phone at 1-877-751-4347